First World War
and Army of Occupation
War Diary
France, Belgium and Germany

46 DIVISION
Divisional Troops
Divisional Ammunition Column
1 February 1915 - 30 June 1919

WO95/2675/3

The Naval & Military Press Ltd
www.nmarchive.com
Published in association with The National Archives

Published by

The Naval & Military Press Ltd

Unit 10 Ridgewood Industrial Park,

Uckfield, East Sussex,

TN22 5QE England

Tel: +44 (0) 1825 749494

www.naval-military-press.com

www.nmarchive.com

This diary has been reprinted in facsimile from the original. Any imperfections are inevitably reproduced and the quality may fall short of modern type and cartographic standards.

© **Crown Copyright**
Images reproduced by permission of The National Archives, London, England, 2015.

Contents

Document type	Place/Title	Date From	Date To
Heading	WO95/2675/3 Divisional Ammunition Column		
Miscellaneous			
Heading	N.M. Division 1st N.M. Divl: ann Col Vol II 1-31.3.15		
War Diary		01/03/1915	31/03/1915
Miscellaneous	Statement.	31/03/1915	31/03/1915
Heading	46th Divl. Ammn Coln Vol III 1-30.4.15		
War Diary		01/04/1915	30/04/1915
Miscellaneous	Statement	01/05/1915	01/05/1915
Heading	46th Division 46th Divl: Ammn Coln Vol IV 1-30.5.15		
War Diary		01/05/1915	30/05/1915
Miscellaneous	Statement	01/06/1915	01/06/1915
Heading	46th Division 46th Divl: Ammn Coln Vol V June 1915		
War Diary		01/06/1915	30/06/1915
Miscellaneous	Statement	30/06/1915	30/06/1915
Heading	46th Division 46th Divl: Ammn Coln Vol VI 1-30-7-15		
War Diary		01/07/1915	30/07/1915
Miscellaneous	Statement		
Heading	46th Division 46th Divl: Ammn Coln Vol VII 1-31.8.15		
War Diary		01/08/1915	31/08/1915
Miscellaneous	Statement.	01/09/1915	01/09/1915
Heading	46th Division 46th Divl: Ammn Coln Vol VIII Sep 1 15		
War Diary		02/09/1915	23/09/1915
Miscellaneous	Statement.	04/10/1915	04/10/1915
Heading	46th Division 46th Ammunition Col. Oct 1915 Vol IX		
Miscellaneous	Statement.	01/11/1915	01/11/1915
War Diary	46th Div Amtn Column	02/10/1915	30/10/1915
Heading	46th Divl Ammn. Col. Nov. Vol X		
Heading	War Diary of 46. Divl. Amm. Col. From 1st To 30 November 1915		
War Diary		04/11/1915	30/11/1915
Miscellaneous	Statement.	01/12/1915	01/12/1915
Heading	46 Div Amm. Col. Dec. 1915		
Heading	War Diary. 46th Divisional Ammunition Column. December 1st: To 31st: 1915. Vol XI		
War Diary	46th to in amtn column.	01/12/1915	28/12/1915
Heading	46th Div Amm Col Jan 1916 Vol XII		
War Diary	Witterness	04/01/1916	16/01/1916
War Diary	Witterness And Pont Remy	16/01/1916	16/01/1916
War Diary	Pont Remy	17/01/1916	17/01/1916
War Diary	Le Toile	23/01/1916	30/01/1916
Heading	North Midland Division NM Divisional Ammn Coln Vol I 1-28.2.15		
War Diary		01/02/1915	28/02/1915
Miscellaneous		12/03/1915	12/03/1915
Heading	War Diary. Divisional Ammunition Column. February 1st:-29th: 1916 Vol XIII		
War Diary	L'etoile	08/02/1916	16/02/1916
War Diary	Lanches	20/02/1916	22/02/1916
War Diary	Fienvillers	29/02/1916	29/02/1916

Heading	War Diary. 46th: Divisional Ammunition Column March 1st: To 31st: 1916		
War Diary	Fignvillers.	02/03/1916	06/03/1916
War Diary	Monts. En. Ternois.	07/03/1916	11/03/1916
War Diary	Monchy. Breton.	15/03/1916	29/03/1916
Heading	War Diary. 46th: Divisional Ammunition Column April 1st: To 30th: 1916. Vol XV		
War Diary	Villers. Brulin.	01/04/1916	22/04/1916
War Diary	Maisnel. St Pol.	23/04/1916	30/04/1916
Heading	War Diary. Divisional Ammunition Column. May 1st: To 31st: 1916. Vol 16		
War Diary	Maisnel. St. Pol.	01/05/1916	08/05/1916
War Diary	Humbercourt.	10/05/1916	18/05/1916
War Diary	Humbercourt & Grincourt.	22/05/1916	22/05/1916
War Diary	Grincourt.	23/05/1916	31/05/1916
Heading	War Diary. Head Quarters 46th. Divisional Ammunition Column June 1st. To June 30th. 1916. Vol 17		
War Diary	Grincourt.	01/06/1916	24/06/1916
War Diary	Humbercourt	24/06/1916	24/06/1916
War Diary	Gaudiempre	25/06/1916	29/06/1916
Heading	War Diary. 46th: Divisional Ammunition Column. July 1st: To July 31st: 1916. Vol 18		
War Diary	Grincourt.	03/07/1916	03/07/1916
War Diary	Gaudiempre.	04/07/1916	04/07/1916
War Diary	Grincourt.	04/07/1916	05/07/1916
War Diary	Gaudiempre.	11/07/1916	15/07/1916
War Diary	Saulty.	24/07/1916	31/07/1916
Heading	War Diary. 46th: Divisional Ammunition Column. August 1st: To August 31st: 1916. Vol 19		
War Diary	Saulty.	07/08/1916	30/08/1916
Heading	War Diary. 46th: Divisional Ammunition Column. September 1st: To September 30th: 1916. Vol 20		
War Diary	Saulty.	04/09/1916	15/09/1916
War Diary	Mondicourt.	16/09/1916	16/09/1916
War Diary	Coullemont.	18/09/1916	18/09/1916
War Diary	Saulty.	21/09/1916	21/09/1916
War Diary	Sombrin.	22/09/1916	24/09/1916
War Diary	Saulty.	25/09/1916	26/09/1916
Heading	War Diary. 46th: Divisional Ammunition Column. October 1st: To October 31st: 1916. Vol 21		
War Diary	Saulty.	03/10/1916	03/10/1916
War Diary	Gaudiempre	03/10/1916	03/10/1916
War Diary	Warlincourt.	06/10/1916	06/10/1916
War Diary	Saulty.	13/10/1916	19/10/1916
War Diary	Soncamp.	21/10/1916	21/10/1916
War Diary	Saulty.	22/10/1916	30/10/1916
Heading	War Diary 46th. Divisional Ammunition Column Vol 22		
War Diary	Coullemont.	01/11/1916	01/11/1916
War Diary	Saulty.	09/11/1916	25/11/1916
Heading	War Diary. 46th: Divisional Ammunition Column. December 1st: To December 31st: 1916. Vol 23		
War Diary	Saulty.	01/12/1916	03/12/1916
War Diary	Milly.	04/12/1916	27/12/1916
Heading	War Diary. 46th: Divisional Ammunition Column. January 1st: To January 31st: 1917. Vol 24		

War Diary	Henu		01/01/1917	31/01/1917
Heading	War Diary. 46. Divisional Ammunition Column. February 1st: To February 28th: 1917. Vol 25			
War Diary	Henu		06/02/1917	28/02/1917
Heading	War Diary. 46th: Divisional Ammunition Column. March 1st: To March 31st: 1917. Vol 26			
War Diary	Henu		05/03/1917	29/03/1917
War Diary	Lemeillard		30/03/1917	30/03/1917
War Diary	Boubers.		31/03/1917	31/03/1917
Heading	War Diary. 46th: Divisional Ammunition Column. April 1st: To April 30th: 1917. Vol 27			
War Diary	Anvin		01/04/1917	01/04/1917
War Diary	Fontes		02/04/1917	13/04/1917
War Diary	L'Ecleme.		14/04/1917	24/04/1917
War Diary	Fosse Dirr de Bracquemont.		27/04/1917	28/04/1917
War Diary	Bracquemont.		29/04/1917	30/04/1917
Heading	War Diary. 46th: Divisional Ammunition Column May 1st: To May 31st: 1917. Vol 28			
War Diary	Noeux. Les. Mines.		01/05/1917	08/05/1917
War Diary	Houchin.		08/05/1917	30/05/1917
Heading	War Diary. 46th: Divisional Ammunition Column June 1st: To June 30th: 1917. Vol 29			
War Diary	Houchin.		01/06/1917	30/06/1917
Heading	War Diary. 46th: Divisional Ammunition Column. July 1st: To July 31st: 1917. Vol 30			
War Diary	Houchin.		01/07/1917	01/07/1917
War Diary	Le Brebis.		03/07/1917	03/07/1917
War Diary	Houchin		04/07/1917	27/07/1917
Heading	War Diary. 46th: Divisional Ammunition Column. August 1st: To August 31st: 1917. Vol 31			
War Diary	Houchin.		02/08/1917	29/08/1917
Heading	War Diary. 46th: Divisional Ammunition Column September 1st: To September 30th: 1917. Vol 32			
War Diary	Houchin.		02/09/1917	02/09/1917
War Diary	Verquineul		02/09/1917	02/09/1917
War Diary	F20 Cent.		02/09/1917	02/09/1917
War Diary	Verquineul		02/09/1917	30/09/1917
Heading	War Diary. 46th: Divisional Ammunition Column. October 1st: To October 31st: 1917. Vol 33			
War Diary	Verquigneul		03/10/1917	31/10/1917
Heading	War Diary. 46th: Divisional Ammunition Column. November 1st: To November 30th: 1917. Vol 34			
War Diary	Verquigneul		01/11/1917	30/11/1917
Heading	46th. Divisional Artillery. War Diary. December-1917. 46th. Divisional Ammunition Column. R.F.A.			
War Diary	Verquigneul		01/12/1917	31/12/1917
Heading	War Diary. 46th: Divisional Ammunition Column. January 1st: To January 31st: 1918. Vol 36			
War Diary	Verquigneul		01/01/1918	25/01/1918
War Diary	Gonngham		26/01/1918	31/01/1918
Heading	War Diary. 46th: Divisional Ammunition Column. February 1st: To February 28th: 1918			
War Diary	Gonnehem.		01/02/1918	09/02/1918
War Diary	Fontaine Les-Hermans		10/02/1918	10/02/1918
War Diary	Lugy		11/02/1918	28/02/1918

Heading	War Diary. 46th: Divisional Ammunition Column. March 1st: To March 31st: 1918		
War Diary	Lugy	01/03/1918	04/03/1918
War Diary	Nedon	04/03/1918	04/03/1918
War Diary	Amettes	05/03/1918	05/03/1918
War Diary	Vendin-Les-Bethune	06/03/1918	29/03/1918
War Diary	Hoduain	30/03/1918	31/03/1918
Heading	46th Divisional Artillery. 46th Divisional Ammunition Column R.F.A. April 1918		
War Diary	Houchin	01/04/1918	12/04/1918
War Diary	Maisnil-Lez Ruitz	13/04/1918	24/04/1918
War Diary	Gosnay	25/04/1918	30/04/1918
Miscellaneous	46th. Division., S.A.A. Section.		
Heading	War Diary. 46th: Divisional Ammunition Column May 1st: To May 31st: 1918		
War Diary	Gosnay	01/05/1918	30/06/1918
Heading	War Diary. Divisional Ammunition Column July 1st: To July 31st: 1918		
War Diary	Gosnay.	01/07/1918	31/07/1918
Heading	War Diary 46th: Divisional Ammunition Column. August 1st: To 31st: 1918		
War Diary	Gosnay.	01/08/1918	12/09/1918
War Diary	Bonnay.	13/09/1918	18/09/1918
War Diary	Mons.	19/09/1918	24/09/1918
War Diary	Cartigny.	25/09/1918	27/09/1918
War Diary	Beaumetz	28/09/1918	29/09/1918
War Diary	Corlancourt.	30/09/1918	30/09/1918
Heading	War Diary. 46th: Divisional Ammunition Column. October 1st: To October 31st: 1918		
War Diary	Caulancourt.	01/10/1918	02/10/1918
War Diary	Pontru.	03/10/1918	09/10/1918
War Diary	Levergies	10/10/1918	11/10/1918
War Diary	Fresnoy-Le-Grand	12/10/1918	01/11/1918
War Diary	Bohain.	02/11/1918	03/11/1918
War Diary	Molain.	04/11/1918	05/11/1918
War Diary	Reset De. Beaulieu.	06/11/1918	06/11/1918
War Diary	Mazieres.	07/11/1918	07/11/1918
War Diary	Prisches.	08/11/1918	09/11/1918
War Diary	Cartignies.	10/11/1918	14/11/1918
War Diary	Landreges	15/11/1918	20/02/1919
War Diary	Quievy.	21/02/1919	28/06/1919
War Diary	Bethencourt	29/06/1919	30/06/1919

WO95/2675/13
Divisional Ammunition Column

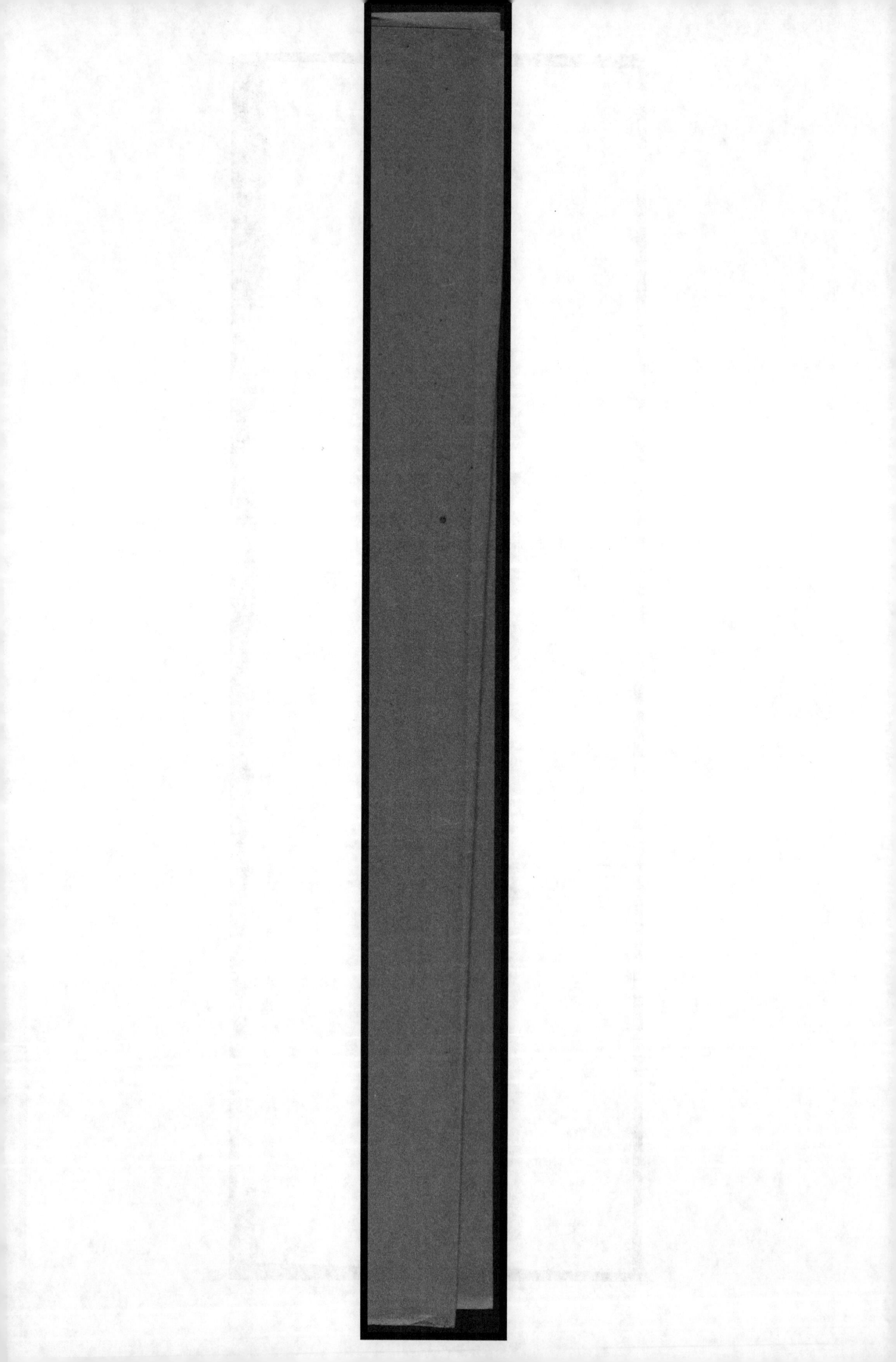

WAR DIARY
or
INTELLIGENCE SUMMARY

(Erase heading not required.)

Army Form C. 2118.

Hour, Date, Place	Summary of Events and Information	Remarks and references to Appendices
GOSNAY. 14:8:18	2/Lt. W.H. JESSOP, 2/Lt. W.N. SCOTT & a/Lt. F.E. AMOS. from S.R. Army Artillery School.	a.o.
" 15:8:18	A/Lt. C.E. RUDGE attd. 231. Brigade. R.F.A.	a.o.
" 16:8:18	A/Lt. W.N. SCOTT, and a/Lt. F.E. AMOS. posted to 230. Brigade R.F.A. 2/Lt. W.H. JESSOP posted to 231 Bde. R.F.A.	a.o.
" 17:8:18	12 Remounts received from Base. 6 L.D. to 230 Brigade R.F.A. 6 " " 231. "	a.o.
" 18:8:18	Lt. J.H. WADDINGHAM. M. commce. at XIII Corps Gas School.	a.o.
" 19:8:18	Lieut. C.E. RUDGE from 231 Brigade R.F.A. to A.A.G Lieut. S.A. JARDINE and a/Lt. I.L. REID. from Advanced Indian Base Depot ROUEN.	a.o.
" 20:8:18	Routine	
" 21:8:18	Routine	
" 22:8:18	Routine	a.o.
" 23:8:18	2/Lt I.L REID proceeds to THEROUANNE to collect Remounts. N. Care at. A/Lt Rodie Elliott. nie falls Indian Personnel.	a.o.

Army Form C. 2118.

WAR DIARY
or
INTELLIGENCE SUMMARY.
(Erase heading not required.)

Instructions regarding War Diaries and Intelligence Summaries are contained in F.S. Regs., Part II. and the Staff Manual respectively. Title pages will be prepared in manuscript.

Place	Hour, Date	Summary of Events and Information	Remarks and references to Appendices
GOSNAY	24.8.18	2/Lt. I.L. REID returned with Recruits and detailed same to Brigades R.A.C.	—
"	25.8.18	Lieut. R.S. ARROWSMITH attached to 230 Brigade R.F.A.	—
"	26.8.18	Lieut. G.G. DAWSON attached to 231 Brigade R.F.A.	—
"	27.8.18	8 L.D. Horses rec'd as reinfs to 230 Bde. 4 to 231 Bde. 4 to 231 Rebn. Routine.	—
"	28.8.18	12 Reinforcements from 5th Army R.A. Reinforcement Camp and distributed as follows:— 7 O.Rs to 230. Bde. R.F.A. – 3 O.Rs to 231 Rebn. 2 O.Rs to R.A.C.	—
"	29.8.18	2/Lts. W.E. Nagle, W.H. Mullis, W.E. House, M.G. Jones, from 5th Army R.A. Camp reported to R.A.C. from 2/Lt. W.H. Mullis posted to A.O. Col.	—
"	30.8.18	2/Lt. W.E. Wright and 2/Lt. W.H. Mullis posted to A.O. Col.	—
"	"	2 /Lt. W.E. House posted to 230 Bde R.F.A. " M.G. Jones posted to 231. Bde R.F.A.	—
"	31.8.18	Routine.	—

(73989) W4141—463. 400,000. 9/14. H.&J.Ltd. Forms/C. 2118/10.

WAR DIARY
or
INTELLIGENCE SUMMARY.
(Erase heading not required.)

Army Form C. 2118.

Hour, Date, Place	Summary of Events and Information	Remarks and references to Appendices
	The following Ammunition has been issued to Batteries during the month: 	A.	B.X.	A Smoke	R.W.C.
---	---	---	---
32,178.	27,678.	13,652.	290.	1100. | There is nothing special to report upon. Remounts and reinforcements arriving during the month have been of good stamp. Discipline has been very good. Health of troops is good. Supplies adequate.	
1.9.16		Nullan Major RHA Comdg 4th Bde. RHA

19

46 D Amm Col CRE

WAR DIARY
or
INTELLIGENCE SUMMARY.
(Erase heading not required.)

Army Form C. 2118.

Hour, Date, Place	Summary of Events and Information	Remarks and references to Appendices
GOSNAY. 1.9.18.	Routine	
2.9.18.	1 Rdr. S.A.A. Satin wounded by hostile shell fire. 1 Mule killed and 5 mules wounded by hostile shell. fire. S.A.A. Sect.	(1) (2)
3.9.18.	Lt. S.A. Lushine to England 14 days leave.	(1)
4.9.18.	19 Reinforcements received from 5th Army R.A. School and distributed to Brigades + T.M. Btys. T. & T.M. held on No. 820,652 Bdr. Mellor T. (Sect. 9 (1) f. A.A)	(1) (2) (3)
5.9.18.	Lt. A. Nash to England 14 days leave.	(1)
6.9.18.	GAME-SPUR dump handed over to 55" D.A.Col. WILSON DUMP handed over to 19" M.T. Coy.	(1) (2)
7.9.18.	Lt. C.E.K. Rudge to Hospital.	(1)
8.9.18.	2/Lt. G.G. Dawson from 231 Bde. RFA. to SACE.	(1)
9.9.18.	No. R.S. Ammsmith " 230 " " "	(1)
10.9.18.	Routine	
11.9.18.	Lt. C.E.K. Rudge from Hospital. Lt. H. Spalding to England 14 days leave.	(1)

Army Form C. 2118.

WAR DIARY
INTELLIGENCE SUMMARY.
(Erase heading not required.)

Instructions regarding War Diaries and Intelligence Summaries are contained in F. S. Regs., Part II. and the Staff Manual respectively. Title pages will be prepared in manuscript.

Hour, Date, Place	Summary of Events and Information	Remarks and references to Appendices
GOSNAY 12.9.18.	H.Qs. Abn. B.A.Col. moved from GOSNAY and entrained at LILLERS. Section 1. moved from GOSNAY and entrained at CALONNE-RICOUART. Section 2. moved from GOSNAY and entrained at CHOQUES. S.A.A. Section moved from BOIS-DE-MONTAIGNES and entrained at LILLERS.	(1)
BONNAY 13.9.18.	Abn. Divn. administered by 3rd Corps. 4th Army. H.Qs. Abn. B.A.Col. and Sects. 1 & 2. detrain at HEILLY and move to BONNAY. S.A.A. Section detrain at HEILLY and remain there.	(1)(2)
14.9.18.	Routine	
15.9.18.	Routine	
16.9.18.	H.Qs. Section 1 & 2. move from BONNAY to CURLU.	(1)(2)
17.9.18.	H.Qs. move from CURLU to BONNAY. Sects. 1 & 2. move with 230 & 231 Bdes R.F.A. to 4th & 12th Dn. Wagon refill.	(1)(2)
18.9.18.	Remount Party, 17 O.Rs. from S.A.A. Section proceed to PLATEAU Rennes.	(1)

Army Form C. 2118.

WAR DIARY
INTELLIGENCE SUMMARY.
(Erase heading not required.)

Instructions regarding War Diaries and Intelligence Summaries are contained in F. S. Regs., Part II. and the Staff Manual respectively. Title pages will be prepared in manuscript.

Hour, Date, Place	Summary of Events and Information	Remarks and references to Appendices
18. 9.18. BONNAY.	S.A.A. Section move from HEILLY to LA-MOTTE.	(W)
19. 9.18. MONS	Hhs. move from BONNAY to MONS. S.A.A. Section move from LA-MOTTE to MONS. Remounts arrive.	(W)
20. 9.18. "	S.A.A. Section move from MONS to BEAUMETZ.	(W)
21. 9.18. "	Routine.	
22. 9.18. "	Change from Bde. Cnfr. to gn Cnfr. 4n Army. Lt. S.A. Gardner proc. on leave to England. Lt. A. Nash " " "	(W)
23. 9.18. "	2 riders + 11. L.D. (Remounts) taken on. Strength of S.A.A. Section 10. L.D. Remounts to 231. Bde. R.t.P. 9. L.D. " " 230 " "	(W)
24. 9.18. "	2/Lt. G.G. Dawson to England. 14 days leave. 1 Riding horse. (Sect. 1) rendered unserving return from Yn. 12n Div. especially to move to ORTIGNY. (BRUSLE)	(W)

WAR DIARY

INTELLIGENCE SUMMARY

(Erase heading not required.)

Army Form C. 2118.

Instructions regarding War Diaries and Intelligence Summaries are contained in F.S. Regs., Part II. and the Staff Manual respectively. Title pages will be prepared in manuscript.

Hour, Date, Place	Summary of Events and Information	Remarks and references to Appendices
25.9.18. CARTIGNY	HQrs. move from MONS to CARTIGNY.	
26.9.18. "	Lt. 20. Allen to England for 14 days leave.	
27.9.18. "	Lt. S. H. Hodinson returns to England for 14 days leave.	
28.9.18. BEAUMETZ	HQrs. move from CARTIGNY to BEAUMETZ. Sect. 2 " " " BRUSLE " Q.A.A. Sect " " BEAUMETZ " MONTIGNY Farm. Sect. 1. " " " CARTIGNY " CORLAN COURT.	
29.9.18. "	I.O.L.D. from Sect. R. and S.L.D. from S.A.A. Sect. transferred to 230 R.R.R.A. H.Qrs and Section 2. move from BEAUMETZ to CORLAN COURT.	
30.9.18. CORLANCOURT.	S.A.A. Sect. move from MONTIGNY Farm to ASCENSION Farm.	

WAR DIARY
or
INTELLIGENCE SUMMARY.
(Erase heading not required.)

Army Form C. 2118.

Hour, Date, Place	Summary of Events and Information	Remarks and references to Appendices
	As will be seen from the diary, many moves have taken place, consequent on the change of the Division from the 5th to the 4th Army, and the successful operation of the Division in attacking the HINDENBURG Line and the crossing of the ST. QUENTIN CANAL. Much work was performed by the Unit in collective ammunition, forward dumps, and the consolidation of same. to forward gun positions. Section 1 F.A. were previous to the above operations attached to the 14th & 12th Divisions with the 230 and 231 Bdes. R.F.A. respectively, to assist in an operation carried out by these Divisions. It is to be recorded that during the operation the good working qualities of the mules was noticeable. Compared with those of the horses. Both the discipline of the troops during the month have been very good. Reinforcements & Remounts have been of good stamp. Supplies adequate.	

Murdoff
Major R.F.A.
Commdg 46° D. A. Cue.

CONFIDENTIAL.

WAR DIARY.

46th: DIVISIONAL AMMUNITION COLUMN.

OCTOBER 1st: to OCTOBER 31st: 1918.

****

Army Form C. 2118.

WAR DIARY
or
INTELLIGENCE SUMMARY.
(Erase heading not required.)

Instructions regarding War Diaries and Intelligence Summaries are contained in F. S. Regs., Part II. and the Staff Manual respectively. Title pages will be prepared in manuscript.

VOL 5

Place	Date	Hour	Summary of Events and Information	Remarks and references to Appendices
CAULANCOURT	1.10.18		Routine	
	2.10.18		Routine	
PONTRU	3.10.18		HQrs. Section 1 & 2 move from CAULANCOURT to PONTRU.	(1)
"	4.10.18		Routine	(2)
"	5.10.18		3 mules of Section 1. wounded by hostile shell fire at Battery position.	(3)
"	6.10.18		Remount party to PERONNE for remounts.	(4)
"	7.10.18		Remounts received. 22 L.D. to 230 Bde. R.F.A. - 16 mules to Section 1.	(5)
			2.H.S. Q.F. majors, 1 G.S. major. 2. N.C.O's & O.R's 20 animals attached to D/230 Bde R.F.A. for attachment to a Cavalry Division.	
"	8.10.18		S.A.A. Section 4to D.A.C. move from ASCENSION FARM to MAGNY-LA-FOSSE.	(6)
"	9.10.18		2/Lt J. REID to ENGLAND. 14 days leave.	(7)
			Section. 1. move from PONTRU to LEVERGIES.	
			" 2 " " " " to BELLENGLISE.	
			SAA Sect " " " " MAGNY-LA FOSSE to MERCOURT.	
LEVERGIES	10.10.18		HQrs. move from PONTRU to LEVERGIES.	(8)
			Section 2 " " LEVERGIES to BEAUREGARD.	
			" 2 " " BELLENGLISE to LEVERGIES.	
"	11.10.18		Section. 2. move from LEVERGIES to BEAUREGARD.	(9)
			H.Qrs. move from LEVERGIES to FRESNOY-LE-GRAND.	

A 5834 Wt. W4973/M687 750,000 8/16 D. D. & L. Ltd. Forms/C.2118/13

WAR DIARY
or
INTELLIGENCE SUMMARY.
(Erase heading not required.)

Army Form C. 2118.

Instructions regarding War Diaries and Intelligence Summaries are contained in F. S. Regs., Part II. and the Staff Manual respectively. Title pages will be prepared in manuscript.

Place	Date	Hour	Summary of Events and Information	Remarks and references to Appendices
PRESNOY-LE-GRAND	12/10/18		2/Lt. G.G. DAYSON from leave to England.	(a)
	13/10/18		Lieut. E. ALLEN " " "	(a)
	14/10/18		Lieut. E. ALLEN + 10. O.Rs. to ROISEL for Remounts.	
	15/10/18		Lieut. J.A. WADDINGHAM M.C. from leave to England.	
			Capt. J.B. MURPHY " " "	(a)
	16/10/18		100 Remounts (L.D) arrive and distributed to Bdes. + D.A.Col.	(a)
	17/10/18		Capt. J.M. THURSFIELD to ENGLAND) 14 days leave.	(a)
	18/10/18		Routine	(a)
	19/10/18		Capt. W. SAVORY M.C. to England. 14 days leave.	(a)
			Capt. W.T. WOOD. R.A.M.C. from leave to England.	
	20/10/18		Routine	
	21/10/18		Capt. H. PAYNE to England (14 days leave)	
	22/10/18		Routine	
	23/10/18		Routine	
	24/10/18		Routine	
	25/10/18		Routine	
	26/10/18		2/Lt. J. REID from leave to England.	(a)
	27/10/18		Routine	
	28/10/18		Routine	
	29/10/18		Routine	

WAR DIARY
or
INTELLIGENCE SUMMARY.
(Erase heading not required.)

Army Form C. 2118.

Place	Date	Hour	Summary of Events and Information	Remarks and references to Appendices
FREMY-LE-GRAND	30/9/16 3/9/18		Ruulis LIEUT. E. ALLEN. + 2/LT. DAWSON. attached to 230. Bde R.F.A. from 46. D.R.C. (1) The following Ammun. has been o/s to Batteries during the month. A.A. — R.A. — A. Smoke 12,975 — 4172 — 500 13,576 During the period under review there is nothing special to report. The training has been in accord. with the greater part of the month. This Unit has arrived the Batteries to salvo Ammun. from forward areas and deliver same to A.R.P's. Training has been undergone in Signalling, Driving Drill &c. Relieves have been given in the evening's by Section Cmdrs. to all ranks. Recruits arriving during month, were of good stamp. Health of Troops. Excellent. Discipline Excellent. Supplies adequate.	(1)

M Nelson
Major R.F.A.
Comdg. 46. R.F.A. C.D.

1/14
46D Army Form C. 2118.

WAR DIARY
or
INTELLIGENCE SUMMARY.
(Erase heading not required.)

Hour, Date, Place	Summary of Events and Information	Remarks and references to Appendices
FRESNOY-LE-GRAND. 1.11.18.	HQrs. 46th R.A.Col. move from FRESNOY-LE-GRAND to BOHAIN.	
BOHAIN. 2.11.18.	Section 1 move from BEAUREGARD FARM to ST. MARTIN-RIVIERE. Section 2 move from BEAUREGARD FARM to ST. MARTIN-RIVIERE.	Rw Rw
" 3.11.18.	Capt. M. Savoy M.C. and 2/Capt. H. Thurgood from leave to England.	Rw
	S.A.A. Section move from BOHAIN to BELLEVUE.	Rw
MOLAIN. 4.11.18.	HQrs. 46th R.A.Col. move from BOHAIN to MOLAIN.	Rw
" 5.11.18.	HQrs. 46th D.A.Col. move from MOLAIN to REJET-DE-BEAULIEU. Section 1 & 2 move from MARTIN-ST. RIVIERE to REJET-DE-BEAULIEU.	Rw
REJET DE BEAULIEU. 6.11.18.	S.A.A. Section move from BELLEVUE to CATILLON. HQrs. 14th R move from REJET-DE-BEAULIEU to MAZIERES. S.A.A. Section move from CATILLON to LA-GROISE.	Rw Rw Rw

WAR DIARY
or
INTELLIGENCE SUMMARY.
(Erase heading not required.)

Army Form C. 2118.

Instructions regarding War Diaries and Intelligence Summaries are contained in F.S. Regs., Part II. and the Staff Manual respectively. Title pages will be prepared in manuscript.

Hour, Date, Place		Summary of Events and Information	Remarks and references to Appendices
MAZIERES.	7.11.18.	Hdrs. from MAZIERES. to PRISCHES. SECTS. 1 & 2. move from MAZIERES. to ERRHART. 3 A.A. Sectn. move from LA GROISE to HAYETTES.	(w)
PRISCHES	8.11.18.	Capt. H. Payne from leave to England. Sect. 2. move from ERRHART. to PETIT FAYT. A. Gunniston to England. 14 days leave.	(w) (w) (w)
"	9.11.18.	Hdrs. How D.A.C. move from PRISCHES. to CARTIGNIES. Sect. 1. move from ERRHART. to CARTIGNIES.	(w) (w)
CARTIGNIES	10.11.18.	LIEUT. E. ALLEN. to D.A.C. from 230. Bde. R.F.A.	(w)
"	11.11.18.	Hostilities cease 11 a.m. Armistice signed. Sect. 2. move from PETIT. FAYT. to ZOREES. 3.A.A. Sect. move from HAYETTES. to ZOREES.	(w)
"	12.11.18.	Routine.	
"	13.11.18.	Routine.	
"	14.11.18.	Lt. C.H. Balme. to D.A.C. from Hospital	(w)

Army Form C. 2118.

WAR DIARY
INTELLIGENCE SUMMARY.
(Erase heading not required.)

Instructions regarding War Diaries and Intelligence Summaries are contained in F.S. Regs., Part II. and the Staff Manual respectively. Title pages will be prepared in manuscript.

Hour, Date, Place	Summary of Events and Information	Remarks and references to Appendices
LANDRECIES 15.11.18.	Sultan 1. and other move— from CARTIGNIES to LANDRECIES. A move from 3 REES 15.	
" 16.11.18.	S.A.A. Bulk move from 3o REES to LE-PREEAU. 9 Riding Horses + G.L.D. from Sultan 1. to 1st INN.	
17.11.18.	2 Mules + G.L.D. from Sult. 2. to 1st INN.	
18.11.18.	Routine.	
19.11.18.	Salvage Scheme Commenced.	
20.11.18.	Educational Scheme Commenced.	
21.11.18.	Routine. Remounts received. 9 mules to Sult 1. 15 " " 2. 6 " " S.A.A. Sect.	
22.11.18.	Routine.	
23.11.18.	1 Officer attached 46th DIVN. to assist with Salvage work.	
24.11.18.	Remounts received. 1 mule to Sect. 1. " " S.A.A. Sect. 13 .	

(73989) W4141—463. 400,000. 9/14. H.&J.Ltd. Forms/C. 2118/10.

Army Form C. 2118.

WAR DIARY
or
INTELLIGENCE SUMMARY.
(Erase heading not required.)

Instructions regarding War Diaries and Intelligence Summaries are contained in F.S. Regs., Part II. and the Staff Manual respectively. Title pages will be prepared in manuscript.

Hour, Date, Place		Summary of Events and Information	Remarks and references to Appendices
LONGUENESSE	25.11.18 26.11.18	Routine. Routine.	
"	27.11.18	2/Lts. T. NELSON & A.V. EDWARDES from England to DAC.	RW
"	28.11.18	Routine.	RW
"	29.11.18	Lt. E.W. Purington from leave to England. Lt. T. Prendman to D.A. Col. from Rouen. A.O.R. to England as Cadet Munro.	RW
"	30.11.18	Routine. This month, man Rouen a Reserve consignment to Armies came into operation on 11th inst. Previous to that date, much work was carried out, delivering ammn. to Battery Positions from the most now uds. Their mus has carried out salvage duties; collecting approx from Pos. 11,000 Rds. S. Ammn. and converging to Cadet Dumps. G.S. wagons and G.S. Limbered wagons have been utilized for this task, & an average of 40 vehicles have been employed daily.	

WAR DIARY
or
INTELLIGENCE SUMMARY.
(Erase heading not required.)

Army Form C. 2118.

Hour, Date, Place	Summary of Events and Information	Remarks and references to Appendices
	Lectures have been attended by Officers & O.R's. on Education during the "Demobilisation" period. Officers have been appointed, to Instruction classes, to benefit the troops in their civil occupations, previous to Scheme 'm' Demobilisation coming into being. The colored list of R.E. Scheme has been carefully explained, and the advantage now, to be relieved in conjunction, has been impressed on all ranks. Health of troops during the month has been good. Discipline excellent. Billets adequate.	William Major R.F.A Comdg. 116 D.A.C.

WAR DIARY
or
INTELLIGENCE SUMMARY.
(Erase heading not required.)

Army Form C. 2118.

46 D Coue Cg 18
Nov. Cg 18

Hour, Date, Place	Summary of Events and Information	Remarks and references to Appendices
HQ RE CIES. 1/12/18.	2g. Runganyeule Addmitted to Brigade aux. SAA Co.	At will be seen from this diary there is nothing to relate for the period under Review. Salvage work has been carried on during the month. In conjunction with the Frances Town Scheme rank 17th Reserve of attending Cambrai, demolishing there, pre war occupations. I have been busy to various workshops to fit them for return to civil life. Rubina Ross Lucy held by Button Coles in Dumbledgekin & Reconciliation schemes, and then...
2/12/18.	Routine	
3/12/18.	Mr. C.H. RAMF SAA Section to Hospitals.	
4/12/18.	Routine	
5/12/18.	Routine	
6/12/18.	Routine	
7/12/18.	Mr C.W.GRIMPTON SAM Section attached for duty to 40th DINN.	
8/12/18.	Routine	
9/12/18.	Routine	
10/12/18.	Routine	
11/12/18.	Routine	
12/12/18.	Routine	
13/12/18.	Routine	
14/12/18.	T. Col. Muirie to CAMBRAI for class II	
15/12/18.	Lt. C. PAXTON. SAM Section to England 10 days leave	
16/12/18.	Lr. R.S. ARROWSMITH. SECT. I " " 30 " "	

WAR DIARY
or
INTELLIGENCE SUMMARY.
(Erase heading not required.)

Army Form C. 2118.

Hour, Date, Place		Summary of Events and Information	Remarks and references to Appendices
VAN DRE CHT.	17.12.18.	Routine	Patients amount
	18.12.18.	Capt. W.T. Ward. R.A.M.C. to England. (Demobilized).	Pargum. Uptains
	19.12.18.	12 Munro's to CAMBRAI for release.	Reinforcements arrived
	20.12.18.	Routine	during month. men of
	21.12.18.	Lt. C.E.K. RUDGE to England. 1st day S. leave	inot. & comp
	22.12.18.	10 Munro's to CAMBRAI for release.	Draughers have been
	23.12.18.	Routine	good.
	24.12.18.	Routine	
	25.12.18.	Routine	Supplies adequate.
	26.12.18.	Routine	
	27.12.18.	Routine	3. Analyse of Wine + men
			dispatched to Engl. (acmt.
	28.12.18.	MAJOR T.R. WILSON. O.C. about D.A.C. to England.	Camp. CAMBRAI on 14th.
		1st day S. leave.	19th. + 22nd inst.
		Arrival of Salvino 1 to 2 - clerified to Emyl	released from military
		+ K. 131. 8 West-Sum. not a Van to disposal	duties to proceed in civil S
		on completion etc.	
	30.12.18.	Lt. E. ALLEN + Lt. P.A. TABIDINE return ?	
		to TOURN. 2nd day S. leave.	
	31.12.18.	Routine	

O.C. 46. R.T.A.

WAR DIARY
or
INTELLIGENCE SUMMARY.

Army Form C. 2118.

Aus Div Am Col

Vol 4 8

Place	Date	Hour	Summary of Events and Information	Remarks and references to Appendices
TINQUES BILLETS	1/11/19		Routine.	
	2/11/19		A.A.V.S. inspects animals of Sect 1 F.R. & 6 D.A.C.	Rec
	3/11/19		Sunday Routine	
	4/11/19		Routine	
	5/11/19		I.A.V.R. inspects animals of Sect 4 F.R. & 6 D.A.C.	Rec
	6/11/19		Routine	Rec
	7/11/19		2/Lt J. Knights 14 days leave to England.	Rec
	8/11/19		A.O.C.R.A. 2nd Army inspects Sections of 46 D.A.C.	Rec
			Lt N Pridman returns from 14 days E. leave to England.	
	9/11/19		Lt. P. A. Allen + Pte S.A. Guthrie returned from 8 days E leave to ROUEN.	Rec
	10/11/19		Inspection of harness of S.a.a. section by S.S.A.V.S.	Rec
	11/11/19		Routine	
	12/11/19		Routine	
	13/11/19		Lt. Col. Myres demobilised.	
			Section 2 of 46 DACol move from HAPPEGARDE to FAVRIL.	Rec

WAR DIARY or INTELLIGENCE SUMMARY.

(Erase heading not required.)

Army Form C. 2118.

Instructions regarding War Diaries and Intelligence Summaries are contained in F. S. Regs., Part II. and the Staff Manual respectively. Title pages will be prepared in manuscript.

Place	Date	Hour	Summary of Events and Information	Remarks and references to Appendices
LANDRECIES	14/1/19		2/Lt. T.A. NASH. 14 days leave to England. Inundation of animals marked X.	No
"	15/1/19		Routine.	
"	16/1/19		2. O.Rs. demobilized.	No
"	17/1/19		Maj. J.R. WILSON. from leave to ENGLAND	
"	18/1/19		4. O.Rs. demobilized.	
"	19/1/19		2. O.Rs. demobilized	No
"	20/1/19		3. O.Rs. demobilized.	
"	21/1/19		1. Officer 4. O.Rs. demobilized.	
"	22/1/19		1. Officer 8. O.Rs. demobilized. Routine.	No
"	23/1/19		1. Officer + 4. O.Rs. demobilized.	
"	24/1/19		3. O.Rs. demobilized.	
"	25/1/19		2. O.Rs. demobilized.	
"	26/1/19		Lt. E.A. ALLEN. 14 days Special leave to ENGLAND. 2/Lt. W. WRIGHT. 14 days " " " "	No

WAR DIARY
or
INTELLIGENCE SUMMARY.

(Erase heading not required.)

Army Form C. 2118.

Places	Date	Hour	Summary of Events and Information	Remarks and references to Appendices
DIEPPE	27/1/19		62 Mules +10 horses to DIEPPE for disposal.	(iv)
"	28/1		P.O.R's demobilised.	
"	29/1		S.O.R's demobilised.	
"	30/1		Anim alt. draught "Y" morphied by DADR when in vain to disposal.	(iv)
"	31/1		19 animals draught "Y" to DIEPPE for disposal.	
			Routine	
			During the month a total of 3 officers 45 O.Rs. have been demobilised, the majority of whom have been drafted men. 89 animals have been evacuated to DIEPPE for disposal of draughrain of draught grain. "G.S" and "Y." G.S. and "Y." Salvage has been carried out during month, a total of 12 nosgm G.S. being employed on this work daily. Health of Troops excellent. Weather in general has been unsettled.	

Wilson Mjn RM
Comdg L of C A.R. Co

Army Form C. 2118.

WAR DIARY
or
INTELLIGENCE SUMMARY
(Erase heading not required.)

49th (N.M.) DIVISION
AMMUNITION COLUMN

Acc. D.A. Col.

Place	Date	Hour	Summary of Events and Information	Remarks and references to Appendices
LANDRECIES	1/2/19		Routine	
	2/2/19		Lieut. M.A. Bashnis (i.e. X & Y) started into D.A. Col.	
	3/2/19		3. O.R.s for demobilization	
	4/2/19		Routine	
	5/2/19		2. O.R.s for demobilization	Ro
	6/2/19		4. O.R.s for demobilization	Ro
	7/2/19		1. O.R. for demobilization	
	8/2/19		4. O.R.s for demobilization	
			Lt. C.A. Balme returned from conducting arrivals for demob.	
	9/2/19		Capt. K. Savoy 1st day's Special leave to England.	Ro
	10/2/19		3. O.R.s for demobilization	
	11/2/19		2/Lt. J. Nash returns from leave to England.	
			Routine	
	12/2/19		2. O.R.s for demobilization	Ro
	13/2/19		2/Lt. C.A. Balme & 4. O.R.s for demobilization	
	14/2/19		Routine	
	15/2/19		Routine	

Army Form C. 2118.

WAR DIARY
or
INTELLIGENCE SUMMARY.
(Erase heading not required.)

Instructions regarding War Diaries and Intelligence Summaries are contained in F.S. Regs., Part II. and the Staff Manual respectively. Title pages will be prepared in manuscript.

Place	Date	Hour	Summary of Events and Information	Remarks and references to Appendices
Army R.O.S.	15/2/19		2/Lt. L. GOLDIE. Proceeds on Course of Gunnery	
	16/2/19		Routine	
	17/2/19		Routine	
	18/2/19		Routine	
	19/2/19		2/Lt. Pinchman returns from 8 days leave to HARVE.	
	20/2/19		H.Qrs. & Section 1. 2. S.A.A. move from LANDRECIES to QUIEVY.	
QUIEVY.	21/2/19		Routine.	
	22/2/19		2/Lt. W.R. Harris transferred from D.A.C. to 230 Bde. R.F.A.	
	23/2/19		Capt. Gascoyne from 14 days leave to England.	
	24/2/19		2/Lt. K.E. Nailer R.E. transfd from D.A.C. to 230. Bde. R.F.A. Assume duties of Adjutant.	
	25/2/19		2/Lt. A.G. Dawson posted to 230 Bde. from D.A.C. Lt. J.H. Hole " " " " " " "	
	26/2/19		2/Lt. O. Glew posted to D.A.C. from 230 Bde. Routine.	

Army Form C. 2118.

WAR DIARY
or
INTELLIGENCE SUMMARY.
(Erase heading not required.)

Instructions regarding War Diaries and Intelligence Summaries are contained in F. S. Regs., Part II. and the Staff Manual respectively. Title pages will be prepared in manuscript.

Place	Date	Hour	Summary of Events and Information	Remarks and references to Appendices
QUIEVY	27/2/19	Routine	There is nothing special to report on, during period under Review. Salvage work has been carried out during month, an average of 12 vehicles daily being emptied. 2 Officers + 4 S.O.Rs. have been demobilised during month. Health of horses has been good. Acceptable evidence. Supplies – adequate.	
	28/2/19	Routine		

[signatures] Major, Cmdg. U.S.A.G.

WAR DIARY
or
INTELLIGENCE SUMMARY.

(Erase heading not required.)

Army Form C. 2118

Place	Date	Hour	Summary of Events and Information	Remarks and references to Appendices
QUIEVY	1/3/19		Routine	
	2/3/19		Routine	
	3/3/19		All ammunition wagons & SAA carts parked @ CAUDRY. Capt CCT nakers (Chaplain) joined from 1/6th S. Staffords.	
	4/3/19		50 Z mules sent for disposal. 30 Z mules sent to HANDRECIES for sale.	
	5/3/19		1 OR for demobilization	
	6/3/19		Routine	
	7/3/19		2 Z horses and 30 Z mules sent to LE CATEAU for sale.	
	8/3/19		7 OR. sent to 104 AFA Bde. Capt. W Humphrey proceeded on leave. 14 X stokers sent for disposal	
	9/3/19		4 ORs for demobilization. 50 mules for disposal	
	10/3/19		Maj F.J. Strachan sent as Conducting Officer with OR for demobilization. Lt G.C. Konnen rewart joined from 13th Cot Ammun. Pk.	
	11/3/19		Routine	
	12/3/19		2 ORs to 65 AFA Bde. 13 ORs for demobilization	

Army Form C. 2118.

WAR DIARY
or
INTELLIGENCE SUMMARY.

(Erase heading not required.)

Instructions regarding War Diaries and Intelligence Summaries are contained in F. S. Regs., Part II. and the Staff Manual respectively. Title pages will be prepared in manuscript.

Place	Date	Hour	Summary of Events and Information	Remarks and references to Appendices
QUIEVY	13/3/19		40 mules to horses for dispersal	
	14/3/19		3 O.Rs to 104 A.F.A. Bde	Ab
			4 O.Rs to demob camp	
			15 "Z" horses for dispersal	
	15/3/19		Routine	
	16/3/19		12 O.Rs for demobilization	Ab
			10 horses + 155 "X" mules transferred to 46 M.G.B.	
	17/3/19		3 horses for dispersal	
	18/3/19		Routine	
	19/3/19		4 O.Rs for demobilization	
	20/3/19		Routine	
	21/3/19		Routine	
	22/3/19		Routine	Ab
	23/3/19		1 O.R. R.A.M.C. Sgt - volunteer) to 46 M.G.B.	
	24/3/19		10 R. for demobilization	
	25/3/19		Lt G.C. Downer for demobilization	Ab
			Capt. Jb. Murphy from leave	
	26/3/19		Routine	
	27/3/19		Capt C.C.T. Peters (Chaplain) for demobilization	

Army Form C. 2118.

WAR DIARY
or
INTELLIGENCE SUMMARY.
(Erase heading not required.)

Instructions regarding War Diaries and Intelligence Summaries are contained in F. S. Regs., Part II. and the Staff Manual respectively. Title pages will be prepared in manuscript.

Place	Date	Hour	Summary of Events and Information	Remarks and references to Appendices
QUIEVY	28/3/19		Routine	
	29/3/19		2/Lt A Geddie returned from Course of Gunnery	
	30/3/19		Lt. D/Y Gordon returned from England.	
	31/3/19		Routine. During the period under review the unit has been reduced to "Cadre A" and most of the animals have been sent for dispersal. Salvage work has been carried on during the month. 2 Of + 38 ORs have been despatched for demobilization during month. Health of troops has been good. Discipline - excellent Supplies - adequate.	

Minton
Major R.F.A.
Commdg.
46 D.A. Column

Army Form C. 2118.

WAR DIARY
or
INTELLIGENCE SUMMARY.
(Erase heading not required.)

46 D Res Sqn

Instructions regarding War Diaries and Intelligence Summaries are contained in F. S. Regs., Part II. and the Staff Manual respectively. Title pages will be prepared in manuscript.

Place	Date	Hour	Summary of Events and Information	Remarks and references to Appendices
QUIEVY	1/4/19	—	2/Lt J.R. Reid to England on leave. 5 Horses received from R.G.A. (18th Bde.)	
	2/4/19	—	2 "Z" Horses sent for disposal	
	3/4/19	—	Capt J.B. Murphy to COLOGNE as Condg. Offr.	
	4/4/19	—	All vehicles sent to Sum Park CAUDRY. 1 Rider ("Z") to mobile Vet. Section	
	5/4/19	—	48 mules & 1 rider to COLOGNE. 2/Lt A. Goldie to A.P.O. 3 "Z" riders to D.A.P.M. 46 R Division	
	6/4/19	—	Routine	
	7/4/19	—	6 mules to Staging Camp BEAUVOIS. Board of audit met to examine a/cs	
	8/4/19	—	Routine	
	9/4/19	—	Routine	Capt S Hurlingham
	10/4/19	—	Capt Crockett remount attached to form Squadron for "Z" Horse depot proceeds on leave	
	11/4/19	—	Routine	
	12/4/19	—	Capt J.B. Murphy return from COLOGNE.	
	13/4/19	—	Major J.R. Wilson proceeded for dispersal independently	
	14/4/19	—	All Indian personnel white personnel for "Z" Horse depot inspected by O.C. "Z" Horse Depot. 10 R. to Remot Camp.	
	15/4/19	—	Sect moved to QUIEVY & personnel for "Z" Horse Depôt take over billets vacated by Section I	
	16/4/19	—	Lt T.H. McLean struck off strength	
	17/4/19	—	Routine	
	18/4/19	—	Routine	
	19/4/19	—	2/Lt J.R. Reid return from leave to England	

Army Form C. 2118.

WAR DIARY
or
INTELLIGENCE SUMMARY.
(Erase heading not required.)

Instructions regarding War Diaries and Intelligence Summaries are contained in F. S. Regs., Part II. and the Staff Manual respectively. Title pages will be prepared in manuscript.

Place	Date	Hour	Summary of Events and Information	Remarks and references to Appendices
QUIEVY	20/4/19		All British & Indian personnel of "Z" Horse Depot entrained @ CAUDRY for NEUFCHATEL	
	21/4/19		Routine	
	22/4/19		Routine	
	23/4/19		Routine	
	24/4/19		Routine	
	25/4/19		Capt. H. Payne proceeded to Paris on leave.	
	26/4/19		Routine	
	27/4/19		Lt. J. Nash proceeded on leave to U.K. Capt. Fitzwatering temporarily from leave. 10 OR to Demob Camp. 1 Watford Detail sent to England. 12 OR sent to R.F.O.	
	28/4/19		Routine	
	29/4/19		Capt. H. Payne returned from leave to Paris.	
	30/4/19		During the period under review all the animals have been sent for disposal, the remaining vehicles have been parked at CAUDRY. 2 Offrs & 20 OR have been sent for Demobilization. Salvage work has been carried on & the two areas allotted have been completely cleared. Health of troops has been good. Discipline - excellent. Supplies - adequate.	

M. L. Davey Lom
Capt. RFA
a/c "Z" D.H.G.

Army Form C. 2118.

WAR DIARY
or
INTELLIGENCE SUMMARY.
(Erase heading not required.)

46D Aus CPL
9/8/52

Place	Date	Hour	Summary of Events and Information	Remarks and references to Appendices
Quièvy	1/5/19	—	Routine	
	2nd	—	Routine	
	3rd	—	Routine	
	4th	—	Routine	
	5	—	Cadre Establishment of DAC reduced to 4 offrs & 168 ORs. Authy RA 46 Bn Pkt A/864/312. 2/d #5/19	
	6	—	Routine	
	7	—	14 OR's sent for Demob.	
	8	—	Routine	
	9	—	Routine	
	10	—	Routine	
	11	—	1 OR sent for Demob.	
	12	—	Routine	
	13	—	Routine	
	14	—	3 OR's to A.of O. Lieut J.A. Nash returned from Leave.	
	15	—	Routine	
	16	—	Routine	
	17	—	Capt W. Savory MC. to Leave. Lieut J. Strachan to England for Repatriation. Capt. H. Payne assumes duties as O.C. DAC.	
	18	—	Routine	
	19	—	Routine	
	20	—	3 OR's to Demob. Lieut J.A. Nash to Demob. Authy RA 46 Bn Pkt A/864/466.	

Army Form C. 2118.

WAR DIARY
INTELLIGENCE SUMMARY.
(Erase heading not required.)

Place	Date	Hour	Summary of Events and Information	Remarks and references to Appendices
Quiévy	MAY 21st	—	Routine	
	22	—	Routine.	
	23	—	14 OR's to Demob.	
	24	—	Routine	
	25	—	Routine	
	26	—	Routine	
	27	—	1. OR. to England for Repatriation.	
	28	—	Routine	
	29	—	Routine	
	30	—	Routine	
	31	—	Routine	
			During the period under review the Cadre Estab was reduced and 1 Offr & 41 OR's have been sent for Demob. 1 Off & 1 OR to England for Repatriation. Health of the Troops has been good. Discipline - excellent. Supplies - adequate.	

Capt RFA
OC 46th Dale

WAR DIARY
INTELLIGENCE SUMMARY.

(Erase heading not required.)

Army Form C. 2118.

46th DIVISIONAL AMMUNITION COLUMN

Place	Date	Hour	Summary of Events and Information	Remarks and references to Appendices
QUIEVY.	1/6/19	—	Routine. Capt. U. Savary MC returned from Leave.	
	2	—	Routine. Capt. E.A. Paulden MC. to 241 Pow. Coy. YPRES. Gully D.A.G. No. PR/498 (M)
	3	—	Capt. H. Payne awarded the MC & 820018. Sgt. Heiston A.B. awarded M.S.M. Published in the London Gazette. 3-6-19.
	4	—	Routine
	5	—	Routine
	6	—	Routine
	7	—	Routine
	8	—	Routine
	9	—	Routine
	10	—	Routine
	11	—	Routine
	12	—	Routine
	13	—	Routine
	14	—	Routine
	15	—	Routine
	16	—	Cadre of 46 D.A.C. (2 offrs & 102 ors) proceeded to UK. Gully #16 RR. AB 158.
	17	—	Personnel of each Section amalgamated to form Equipment Guard.
	18	—	Routine
	19	—	Routine
	20	—	Routine

WAR DIARY or INTELLIGENCE SUMMARY.

(Erase heading not required.)

Army Form C. 2118.

46th DIVISIONAL AMMUNITION COLUMN

Hour, Date, Place	Summary of Events and Information	Remarks and References to Appendices
GUIVRY 21-6-19	Routine	
22	Routine	
23	Stores etc packed on vehicles & Guards doubled.	
24	Routine	
25	Routine	
26	Routine	
27	Routine	
28	D.A.C Equipment Guard moves to BETHENCOURT.	
Bethencourt 29	Routine	
30	Routine	
	During the period under review, the Cadre left for the UK, and the remainder of the unit assumes the title of Equipment Guard and moving into Bethencourt. Health of the troops has been good. Discipline — Excellent. Supplies — adequate.	

O.C. Coy DG
46th D.A.C.

Army Form C. 2118.

WAR DIARY
INTELLIGENCE SUMMARY
(Erase heading not required.)

Hour, Date, Place	Summary of Events and Information	Remarks and references to Appendices
GOENAY		
1.8.18.	Routine	
2.8.18	Routine	
3.8.18.	Spalding returns from 13th Corps Rest Station.	(a)
4.8.18.	Routine	
5.8.18	Routine	
6.8.18	Routine	
7.8.18.	3 mules each from Sections 2 & S.A.A. Section to M.W.S.	
	1 Officer, 11 O.Rs. (Reinforcements) from S.A. Army R.A.	
	Reinforcement School & distributed as follows:-	
	1 Officer to 1/6 A.T.A.G. 8 O.Rs. to 231 Brigade	
	2 O.Rs. to 1/4 Lo T.M. Bty. 1 O.R. to 1 A. R.A.	(b)
	Lieut. G. E. RUDGE posted to Section 1 from Base.	(c)
	Lieut. G. H. BALME attached to 230 Brigade R+A	(d)
8.8.18.	Routine	
9.8.18.	Routine	
10.8.18.	Routine	
11.8.18	Routine	
12.8.18.	Routine	
13.8.18	Routine	

CONFIDENTIAL

- WAR DIARY -

46th: DIVISIONAL AMMUNITION COLUMN.

AUGUST 1st: to 31st: 1918.

WAR DIARY
INTELLIGENCE SUMMARY.
(Erase heading not required.)

Army Form C. 2118.

Hour, Date, Place	Summary of Events and Information	Remarks and references to Appendices
GIRNAI 28.12.18	Routine.	
" 31.12.18	Routine.	
" 3.1.19	Routine. Major R. Nilson from leave to England. (2) Mules and L.D. to from B.d.66.	
	2 Indian O.R.s. (Reinforcements) from base. Lieut. H.S. Hall R.F.A. attached w.e.f. estab. of 4th Field Survey Battn. (Authy. N.S. S.S/1362(0) 8.16.12.18	
	The following Annexures have been received during the month.	
	A. A.K. B.X. A.Smoke. B.N.G.	
	39,094. 24,289. 16,278. 500. 600.	
	There is nothing of special to report, during the month. Pro-wars have been completed amunt ment dicts, and have standings. Reinforcement and supplies arriving during month were of much savings. Health of troops - good. Mounting - good.	

Major
Comdg. 4th A.F. Coy

Army Form C. 2118.

WAR DIARY
INTELLIGENCE SUMMARY.
(Erase heading not required.)

Instructions regarding War Diaries and Intelligence Summaries are contained in F.S. Regs., Part II and the Staff Manual respectively. Title pages will be prepared in manuscript.

Hour, Date, Place	Summary of Events and Information	Remarks and references to Appendices
13.7.18. GOSNAY.	Lieut. S.A. JARDINE. 2/Lieut. J.L. REID. and 4 N.C.O's to Anti-Gas Course @ Garnier & in R.A. Base Depot.	R/o
14.7.18	2/Lt. G.G. DAWSON. returns from Gas. Course.	
15.7.18	MAJOR. J.R. WILSON. - 14 days leave to England.	R/o
16.7.18	Routine.	
17.7.18	8 reinforcements from 1st Army R.A. Camp and due tonight to Bttys.	R/o
18.7.18	Routine.	R/o
19.7.18	2/Lt H. SPALDING to rest Camp Paris-Plage.	R/o
20.7.18	Hay ration reduced to 9 lbs.	R/o
21.7.18	Routine.	
22.7.18	Routine.	
23.7.18	Routine.	
24.7.18	Lieut R.J. Jocelin (General List) and posted to S.A.A. Section.	R/o
25.7.18	Routine.	
26.7.18	Routine.	
27.7.18	Lieut. S. TURNER. and 2/Lt. W. EMERY attached to 230 Bde. R.F.A.	R/o

WAR DIARY
INTELLIGENCE SUMMARY.
(Erase heading not required.)

Army Form C. 2118.

Hour, Date, Place	Summary of Events and Information	Remarks and references to Appendices
31.2.1	Routine.	
31.2.2	Routine.	
31.2.3	Routine. & reinforcements received & distributed to Brigades 3 to 230 Bde. R.F.A. 15 to 231 Bde R.F.A. Lt. F.S. Arrowsmith returns from leave to England.	
31.2.4	Routine.	
31.2.5	Lt. S.R. Jenkins returns to 4th. STA Gp. from 'K' Anti-Aircraft Battery. 1 Farr. Sgt. to BOULOGNE with Div. Remount party in ambulance.	PW
31.2.6	1 O.Rs. slightly wounded by enemy shell fire. 2/Lt G.G. Dawson proceeds on 14 days Gas Course. 2/Lt A. NASH and 1 O.R. from Anti Indian Base Depot ROUEN (HINDUSTANI COURSE).	PW
31.2.7	Routine. Remounts received from BOULOGNE & distributed as follows:— NA.C 3 to 1 Brigades	PW
31.2.8	Routine.	
31.2.9	Routine.	
31.2.10	Routine.	

CONFIDENTIAL.

WAR DIARY.

DIVISIONAL AMMUNITION COLUMN

JULY 1st, to JULY 31st, 1918.

WAR DIARY
or
INTELLIGENCE SUMMARY
(Erase heading not required.)

Army Form C. 2118.

Place	Date	Hour	Summary of Events and Information	Remarks and references to Appendices
GSNA	29.6.16		19 Indian O.R's (reinforcements) from Basra and distributed as follows. 1 to Section 1. 5 to Section R. 7 to S.A.D. Sadlin. 6 to India.	
"	30.6.16		The following Ammn. has been received during the month.	

A.P. 23,23.   A.M. 9309.   Q.X. 11,100.   A.Smeliv 330.   R.H.E. 1753.   B.Incend. 240.   B.P.S. 122.

During the period under review, there is nothing special to report. No met. important part being the reduction of Ammn. Q. & magazine lines from 6 to 4 Rounds during the month. On completion of Gun fires that has been made during the month, more of Lee standing's and bomb-proof however, move of Reinforcements in men and Remounts arriving during month, are of good stamp.

An epidemic of slight fever affected about 40% of O.R's remaining here in Aziziya for a period of 3 days, the whole health of troops has been good. Supplies received during month have been adequate & Discipline - very good.

M Mclean Major R.A.
Comdg 40th S.A. Col.

Army Form C. 2118.

WAR DIARY
or
INTELLIGENCE SUMMARY.
(Erase heading not required.)

Instructions regarding War Diaries and Intelligence Summaries are contained in F.S. Regs., Part II. and the Staff Manual respectively. Title pages will be prepared in manuscript.

Place	Date	Hour	Summary of Events and Information	Remarks and references to Appendices
Gezira	13.6.18		O.C. 46th DAC reports. Section 2 46th DAC in F.S.M.O.	Red
"	14.6.18		Routine	Red
"	15.6.18		Lt. F.H. Hole (230 Bde R.F.A) posted to this DAC from 15.6.18. 2/Lt. H.T.N. Butler to this DAC " "	Red
"	16.6.18		Routine	Red
"	17.6.18		Routine	Red
"	18.6.18		A.R.P. Ammunition proceeds on 14 days leave to England.	Red
"	19.6.18		R3 Reinforcements distributed to Brigades as follows:- 13 to 230 Brigade R.F.A. 10 to 231 Brigade R.F.A.	Red
"	20.6.18		Routine	
"	21.6.18		Routine	
"	22.6.18		Routine	
"	23.6.18		W.O. field tennis Signal Base kept and recorders to Signal Service (Cavalry) A.G. 52/2133 dated 30.5.18.	Red
"	24.6.18		Routine	
"	25.6.18		Lieut. G.H. Baens returned from leave to England.	Red
"	26.6.18		Routine	
"	27.6.18		Adm. Dvn. Kenjamech from 14 to 14 Corps.	Red
"	28.6.18		Reduction in the estab. of horses taking as follows:- Ammn. O.E. wagon teams to be reduced from 6 to 4 horses. Spare horses increased from 40 to 60 6t. L.O.R's. 16. L.D. to base. 10. O.R's. to 1st Army R.A.R. Camp. Authy. G.H.Q. No. OB/1866 E dated 10.6.1918.	Red

A5834 Wt.W4973/M687. 750,000 8/16 D.D.& L.Ltd. Forms/C.2115/13.

WAR DIARY
or
INTELLIGENCE SUMMARY.
(Erase heading not required.)

Army Form C. 2118.

Vol 41

Place	Date	Hour	Summary of Events and Information	Remarks and references to Appendices
GOSNAY	1.6.18		Routine.	No
"	2.6.18		"	
"	3.6.18		"	
"	4.6.18		"	
"	5.6.18		1 Officer n.o.Rs to Remount Camp, THEROUANNE. Remount 20 uniformed anvis and distributed as follows. 10 to 230. Bde. 6 to 231 " " T.M. Btys. 4 " to sections 2 Remounts.	No
"	6.6.18		Remount Party returned, and remounts distributed 2 mules to 4/h. Div. S. to section 1. 8 to section 2. Routine.	
"	7.6.18		Routine	No
"	8.6.18		Auth. S.G. Sanitary Co. "K" Anti-Aircraft Batty from one month furlough duty. Army Letter no. SS22/S.P. dated 1.6.18 No. 42247. B.Q.M.S. Jones W. 2/h. Brigade R.F.A. appointed to a Gunnery commission via 2/lt and posted to 4th D.A. Col. Auth. A.G. 2159/1165 (o) dated 28.5.18 M. Ed. R. Grimsden. Winner from Leave to England. G.O.C. 4th Divn. instructs baction 1. " D.A. Col. in G.S.M.O.	No
"	9.6.18			No
"	10.6.18			No
"	11.6.18		The following Officers dated as follows. 2/Lt. S.W. BRIDGEWATER } to a/k. W.H.T. HOUTEN } C. JACKSON } 230 Brigade " G. MITCHELL D.C.M. } " N.A. BRAMWELL. } 231 Bde. " H. McLEAN } to 230 Brigade R.F.A. } R+A " T.W. HARPHAM. }	No No
"	12.6.18		Routine.	No

WAR DIARY
or
INTELLIGENCE SUMMARY.
(Erase heading not required.)

Army Form C. 2118.

Place	Date	Hour	Summary of Events and Information	Remarks and references to Appendices
			At the beginning of the month, it will be noticed that B.A.C. come on to W.E. 612. British and Indian Personnel. The late are not so good as British Personnel, the outstanding drawback being they cannot be sent out on any duty unless accompanied by a proportion of white Personnel. There has been no move during the month. A considerable amount of work has been done in improving and rebuilding huts & shacks for men, to enable them to be taken out of the cottages in which they were billeted. Some detrimentals to their health. It is very difficult in the very cold to find the usual fatigue parties for camps, digging, and arrangements for French Indians as in most cases Indian Personnel cannot be used. The B.A.C. should we have at least 20 men over-strength at all times, to provide for these fatigues. Reinforcements and remounts received during month were of good stamp. Discipline has been good. Supplies adequate. Health of Horses good.	

Milton Wyn??
Commanding 46 B.A.C.

Army Form C. 2118.

WAR DIARY
of
INTELLIGENCE SUMMARY.
(Erase heading not required.)

Instructions regarding War Diaries and Intelligence Summaries are contained in F.S. Regs., Part II. and the Staff Manual respectively. Title pages will be prepared in manuscript.

Place	Date	Hour	Summary of Events and Information	Remarks and references to Appendices
GOSNAY	23		2/Lt A. GOLDIE. " C.E. WHITTINGHAM. } posted to 230 Bde RFA 2/Lt W.E. DATE " C.T. CUTHBERT. } posted to 231 Bde. " S.A. WOODLANDS } R.F.A.	A/c A/c
"	24		2/Lt J.H. NADDINGHAM from Hos T.M. Btys to Hd D.A. Col.	A/c
"	25		2/Lt S.A. NASH and 3 O.R's ground to Indian Cavalry Depôt ROUEN (in HINDUSTANI Course).	A/c
"	26		1 Offr 16 O.R's ground to MARLES-LES-MINES for enemy's Lieut E.W GRIMSTON proceeding on 14 days leave to England. 3 O.R. Remounts received and distributed to Brigades.	A/c A/c
"	27		Routine	A/c
"	28		Routine	
"	29		2/Lt E.L. REID from 231 Bde. R.F.A. to Hd D.A. Col.	A/c
"	30		A & transfer. to Hd. H.A.C. from 1 Corps.	A/c
"	31		Routine.	

The following ammunition has been expended during the month.

A	A.X	B.X	A Smoke	B.N.C	B.N.N	B.P.C	B.G.R.R
23,542	12,338	10,960	694	4848	984	152	400

WAR DIARY

INTELLIGENCE SUMMARY

(Erase heading not required.)

Army Form C. 2118.

Place	Date	Hour	Summary of Events and Information	Remarks and references to Appendices
GOENEK	14		Inspection of animals of Section 2 by A.D.V.S.	(0)
"	15		The following reinforcement Officers join from England unit FH Hole. P.E. Amyra. 2/Lts C.E. Sykes, J.C. Burnie	(0)
"	16		Routine	(0)
"	17		R.E. Offensive wagon unit 2 drivers and 4 mules transferred to S.A.A Section from HQrs Staff	(0)
"			Lieut. P.E. Amyra attached to HQ R.A.	
"	18		The following officers posted to Brigades from A.A. Col.	(0)
"			2/Lt. C.E. Sykes } orders to { 2/Lt. H.H. Mogham atts 230 Bde. R+A.	
"			2/Lt. F.H. Hole } 230 Bde. { 2/Lt. J.C. Burnie orders 231 "	
"			2/Lt. H.W. Beeson " " { 2/Lt. G.L. Reeve 231 "	
"	19		2/Lt. E.L. Alexander atts 230 Bde } attached to T.M. Batteries	(0)
"			2/Lt. W.E. Ratevay " 231 " }	
"	20		Routine	(0)
"	21		Following Officers from 1st Army reinforcement camp	(0)
"			2/Lts Goldie atts. Sect 1 } 2/Lt. G.A. Whittingham } atts. Section 2	
"			" J.T. Cuthill atts Sect 1 } J.A. Worthlands	
"			" T.F. Dale " " }	
"	22		Routine	

WAR DIARY
of
INTELLIGENCE SUMMARY.
(Erase heading not required.)

Army Form C. 2118.

Instructions regarding War Diaries and Intelligence Summaries are contained in F. S. Regs., Part II. and the Staff Manual respectively. Title pages will be prepared in manuscript.

Place	Date	Hour	Summary of Events and Information	Remarks and references to Appendices
GOSNAY	23.		2/Lt A. GOLDIE " G.E. WHITTINGHAM } Posted to 230 Bde RFA Lt T.H. WADDINGHAM from 46th T.M. Bty to Hdq D.A. Col.	2/Lt W.E. DATE " G.T. CUTHBERT } Posted to 231 Bde " S.A. WOODLANDS } R.F.A.	No No
"	24.		2/Lt S.A. NASH and 3 O.R's proceed to Indian Cavalry Depot ROUEN for HINDUSTANI Course.	No
"	25.		1 Officer 16 O.R's proceed to MARLES-LES-MINES for inmn'ts Lieut. E.W. GRIMSTON proceeds on 14 days leave the England	No
"	26.		38 Remounts received and distributed to Brigades.	No
"	27. 28.		Routine. Routine.	No No
"	29.		2/Lt M. E.L. REID from 231 Bde. R.F.A. to Hdr D.A. Col. A/Lt Suman to 4th NTAC from 1 Corps.	No
"	30. 31.		Routine.	No

The following ammn. has been received during the month

A.	A.X.	B.X.	A. Smoke.	B.N.C.	B.V.N.	B.P.S.	B.G.R.R.
23,542	12,338	10,960	694	848	489	152	400

WAR DIARY

INTELLIGENCE SUMMARY.

Army Form C. 2118.

Place	Date	Hour	Summary of Events and Information	Remarks and references to Appendices
GOSNEY	14		Inspection of animals	
	15		The following reinforcement Officers join from England halls & H. Hole, P.E. Amyron, 2/Lt. P.E. Sykes, 2/Lt. C. Bunnie	
	16		Routine	
	17		R.E. Officers. wagon, with 2 drivers and 4 mules transferred to S.A.A. Section from H.Qrs. Staff Lieut. P.E. Amyron attached to 14 D.R.A.	
	18		The following officers posted to Brigades from A.A. Col. 2/Lt. C.E. Sykes } join to 2/Lt. H. Mahan attd 230 Bde. R+A W. f. H. Hole } 230 Bde. 2/Lt. C. Bunnie join 231 " A.W. Beeson " " Q.L. Pearce A 31	
	19		Lt. C. Alexander attd 230 Bde } attached to T.M. Batteries 2/Lt. W.E. Ridgway " 231 "	
	20		Routine	
	21		Following Officers join from 1st Army - reinforcement camp 2/Lt. Golan } attd. Sect. 1. 2/Lt. G.H. Whittingham } attd Sections 2 S.T. Curtis H.E. Hole S.A. Woodlands	
	22		Routine	

Army Form C. 2118.

Vol 40

WAR DIARY
or
INTELLIGENCE SUMMARY
(Erase heading not required.)

Place	Date	Hour	Summary of Events and Information	Remarks and references to Appendices
GOSHA	1		British and Indian W. Estab. No. 818 convs into Force & the Itinerary British personnel sent to 1st. Army R.A. reinforcement Camp. 3 Cpls. 2 Cpls. 1. S. Smith. 2. L. Bar. J. & 11 S. Brothers and Rivers. Routine	Ap
	2			Ap
	3		2 Ofrs & 8 O.R's from 1st. Army engagement Camp. and Greek to H.Q. T.M. Bty. 15 O.R's from 1st. Army rein Camp. own Orders to 1014 R.A. Col. Ap Routine	Ap Ap
	4		2/Lt. E. O. HILLYARD. (attd D/230 Bty) obtained map 1st Field. Survey Try R.E. Quadrin disembarkation into Estab (Auth. A.6.55/2093(9).	Ap
	5		Routine	Ap
	6		Routine	
	7			
	8		Lt. J. H. NADDINGHAM. M.C. 2/Lt. D.T. STRACHAN to 40th T.M. Rfs.	Ap
	9		GAME. SPIR. AMMUN DUMP. (K.3.B.2.7) opened Routine	Ap
	10		2/Lt. K. D. ABRAHAMS. gratia from H.Q. D.A.Col. to 231 Bde RFA. 1. O.R. and 1 mule slightly wounded by hostile shell fire whilst delivering ammun. to Batty.	Ap
	11		Routine	Ap
	12			Ap
	13		Inspection of ammun of Section 1 by A.E.V.S.	Ap

CONFIDENTIAL.

WAR DIARY.

46th: DIVISIONAL AMMUNITION COLUMN

May 1st: to May 31st: 1918.

46th. DIVISION.

S.A.A. SECTION.

Numbers 1, 2, and 3 Sub-Divisions.

4 Limbered G.S. Wagons, each carrying 18 boxes S.A.A.,
4 G.S. Wagons each carrying 34 boxes S.A.A.,
1 G.S. Wagon carrying 112 boxes No. 23 Grenades, with rods and ctgs.
1 G.S. Wagon carrying 20 boxes Stokes Mortar Amm'n.
                       1 box Webley Pistol Amm'n.
                       10 boxes Ground Flares, Red.
                       8 boxes V.P.A., 1" White.
                       1 box V.P.A., 1" Red.
                       1 box V.P.A., 1" Green.

Total carried :-

         208,000 rounds S.A.A.,
         1,344 No. 23 Grenades, with rods and cartridges.
         276 rounds Webley Pistol Ammunition.
         480 rounds Stokes Mortar Amm'n.
         2,660 Ground Flares, Red.
         1,200 V.P.A., 1" White.
         150 V.P.A., 1" Red.
         150 V.P.A., 1" Green.

Number 4 Sub-Division.

3 Limbered G.S. Wagons each carrying 18 boxes S.A.A.,
6 G.S. Wagons each carrying 34 boxes S.A.A.,
1 G.S. Wagon carrying 20 boxes S.A.A.,
                       1 box Webley Pistol Amm'n.
                       2 boxes Ground Flares, Red.
                       2 boxes V.P.A., 1" White.
                       Spare barrels.
                       Spare belts.

Total carried :-

         278,000 rounds S.A.A.,
         276 rounds Webley Pistol Ammunition.
         512 Ground Flares, Red.
         300 V.P.A., 1" White.
         Spare Barrels and spare belts as available.

WAR DIARY
or
INTELLIGENCE SUMMARY

Army Form C. 2118.

46th D.A.C.

Place	Date	Hour	Summary of Events and Information	Remarks and references to Appendices
GEZAY			Ammunition issued etc during month	
			A AX BX BNC BVN SAA VPA	
			18,315 1,894 6574 4250 250 337,000 3 Boxes	
			Gas No 5 No 36 No 23	
			9 sets 720 2328	

Signed
Major RA
Comdg 46 DAC

WAR DIARY
or
INTELLIGENCE SUMMARY

Army Form C. 2118.

46th D.A.C.
April 1918

Place	Date	Hour	Summary of Events and Information	Remarks and references to Appendices
Gosnay	29	Routine	During the period under review the 46 D.A.C. has had a real rest from the 16/3/18 to 24/4/18. There were two refittings, the second of which commenced on the 24th. Rearmament was carried out throughout the month. Rearmament has also meant that the monthly returns have been neither very satisfactory or made good. Personnel has been engaged at drill. Rifle S.A.T. before the men were engaged upon a course of Lectures and Sub Courses explaining ammunition & not advanced. B.C. one to the O.M.G. Battn. Diristol Exhibition commenced.	
"	30	Routine	Rifle. Firing of Lewis Gunner in and super. Salute. Over has been carried out along the month in number long erected by Sunday. Supplies are & released. Purchases very good. Health of personnel has been very good during the month.	

WAR DIARY
or
INTELLIGENCE SUMMARY.
(Erase heading not required.)

Army Form C. 2118.

46 D A C
23/Feb 1918

Place	Date	Hour	Summary of Events and Information	Remarks and references to Appendices
MAISNIL LES RUITZ	15		Personnel & Rolls steward from THEROUANNE & renewals distributed as follows	—
			6 O.R. to Sections E	—
	16		H Reinforcement from DIV. DEPOT BATT:N	—
	17		Reinforcements distributed as follows. 1 R.E. N.C.O. 46 D.A.C	—
			R.F.A. 6 O.R. to 46 D.A.C. 1 O.R. 1 Br. 250 Bde R.F.A. 1 O.R. 251 Bde	—
"	18		ROUTINE	—
"	19		ROUTINE	—
"	20		ROUTINE	—
"	21		2 Officers, 56 O.R., 82 animals, 15,115 Rds S.A.A, 6 G.S. wagons attached to 50th DAC	—
"	22		1 Officer, 58 O.R. proceed to MARLES-LES-MINES for Remounts	—
"	23		In the Village Personnel received charges & details & details distributed to H.Q. & Sect	—
			Detailed half strength from 50th DAC	—
	24		1 Br. Sect. 1 LtY S.A.A. move from MAISNIL LES RUITZ to GOSNAY	—
			2 NDR ST REED & RET:N S LAST finished to B:ARMY Bde R.F.A.	—
	25		S.A.A. Sect. 46 D.A.C. move from Gosnay to E. of outskirts of may/stad 36B	—
GOSNAY	26		2 ND LT B.V. O'CONNOR to ENGLAND. Sect: 16/4/18. LT E. ALLEN from 46 T.M. B:Y	—
			to Sect 1 46 D.A.C. 2 ND LT J.C. GILLES PIE to 46 T.M. B:Y from S.A.A. Sect	—
"	27			—
"	28		1 O.R. & 2 MULES command by 50th DAC well 46	—
			ROUTINE	—

Army Form C. 2118.

Instructions regarding War Diaries and Intelligence Summaries are contained in F. S. Regs., Part II. and the Staff Manual respectively. Title pages will be prepared in manuscript.

46th D.A.C.

April 1918

Vol 39

WAR DIARY
INTELLIGENCE SUMMARY.
(Erase heading not required.)

Place	Date	Hour	Summary of Events and Information	Remarks and references to Appendices
HOLNON	1		Capt W Shutts M.O.R.C. left base	[ref]
	2		Resting	[ref]
	3		Resting	[ref]
	4		Roth Barnet SAA Subsvund from Holnon to Fossa Dith Dupont	[ref]
	5		Resting	[ref]
	6		Resting	[ref]
	7		Resting	[ref]
	8		The following officers sent home to England. 2nd Lts S.T. Reed - at last	[ref]
	9		Resting	[ref]
	10		Resting	[ref]
	11		" Reformed from D.A.C. Depot Batt.	[ref]
			Battalions distributed as follows: 6th 230 Bde. 2nd 231 Bde. 100 Tns S.A.C.	[ref]
			HQ & Section. 1st & 2nd SAA Sections 6th (Right Barrel) more by Holnon	[ref]
			to Maisnil-lez-Ruitz. 2nd Section SAA Subsvund from Fosse Dith	[ref]
			Dupont to Maisnil-lez-Ruitz.	[ref]
MAISNIL-LEZ	12		Entrained to MVS	[ref]
RUITZ	13		Rect Col Edward of SAA Brigades left to Join 31st SAA Subsvund	[ref]
			Capts S.T. Reed & A. Leaft attached to 231 Bde RFA	[ref]
	15		2nd Lt SA Jardine May 231 Bde RFA to 46 D.A.C.	[ref]
			& Capt J.C. Gilks RFA from 46 S.M. Bde left D.A.C.	[ref]

46th Divisional Artillery.

46th DIVISIONAL AMMUNITION COLUMN R.F.A.

APRIL 1918.

Instructions regarding War Diaries and Intelligence Summaries are contained in F. S. Regs., Part II. and the Staff Manual respectively. Title pages will be prepared in manuscript.

WAR DIARY
or
~~INTELLIGENCE SUMMARY.~~
(Erase heading not required.)

46th D A C
March 1918

Army Form C. 2118.

Place	Date	Hour	Summary of Events and Information	Remarks and references to Appendices
HOUCHIN.			During the period under review the Division moved from rest Area into Action, the following amounts of ammunition has been supplied by D A C 25841 A, 20120 AX, 10193 BX. Several Officers have joined during the month & attached to Brigades. Much work has been done during the month to improve horse standings & billets. Indian Personnel have received instruction in all duties of a British driver, & have made satisfactory progress. Reinforcements arriving during the month have been of good physique & good stamp generally. Remounts arriving during the month have been a fair stamp. Supplies have been adequate, health of troops excellent. During the month instruction has been given to N.C.O.s & men in Map reading, manipulation of Box respirators both by day & night. [illegible] Major R.F.A Comdg 46th D.A.C	

A5834 Wt. W4973/M687 750,000 8/16 D. D. & L. Ltd. Forms/C.2118/13.

WAR DIARY or INTELLIGENCE SUMMARY

Army Form C. 2118.

46th D.A.C.

March 1918

Place	Date	Hour	Summary of Events and Information	Remarks and references to Appendices
VENDIN LES BETHUNE	25		6.0 a.m. To BOULOGNE for renewal	
			2nd Lt. A W MILHOLLAND from 46th D.A.C. to 61st Div, 2nd Lt. J.O. GILLESPIE from T.M. Bty.	
	26		2nd Lt. J A NASH from 46th T.M. Bgs to SAA Sec Ell	
			Sec I 46th D.A.C. moved from AMETTES to GONNEHEM	
			12 teams sent away from 46 Div Depot Batt.	
	27		Routine	
	28		Routine. Established influenza through to 230 Bde & 231 Bde, 12th & 46th D.A.C. Rec'd SAA. Began taking out to SAA Sec McGOVERN. DUMP OFFADIA following gun ammunition dumps A Field, BANKS, DUMP,	
			GARDEN DUMP, MUSHROOM DUMP brought out to 11 Bde. TOADSTOOL DUMP handed over to 55th Div	
	29		H'Qrs & Sec II moved from VENDIN-LES-BETHUNE to HOUCHIN Sec I moved from GONNEHEM to HOUCHIN SAA Sec move from Lt. QUESNOY to HOUCHIN	
HOUCHIN	30	10	Renewat received from BOULOGNE, distributed troops to Sections I, SAA Undermentioned Officers posted to Bdes with effect from date shown 2nd Lt R W T JONES } to 230 Bty } Lieut R J MARKHAM } to 231 Bty Ell 2nd Lt C P BURGIES } 25 inst } Lieut D A CARR 25 inst	
	31		Routine	

Army Form C. 2118.

46th D.A.C.
March 1918

WAR DIARY
or
INTELLIGENCE SUMMARY.

(Erase heading not required.)

Place	Date	Hour	Summary of Events and Information	Remarks and references to Appendices
VENDIN-LES-BÉTHUNE	14		2nd Lt N.A. BRAMWELL att. 231 Bde R.F.A. to 46th T.M. B?	
	15		2nd Lt A.D.K. THIMPSON att. 230 Bde R.F.A to 46th T.M. B?	
			2nd Lt D.K. ABRAHAMS to 46 D.A.C. from ENGLAND. 40 O.Rs to BOULOGNE. Remained posts	
	16		3 mules from S.A.A. Sect. 46 D.A.C. to A.M.V.S.	
	17		Lt C.H. BAINE to 46 D.A.C. from hospital. 18 Reinforcements received	
	18		Reinforcement detailed as follows. 4 O.Rs, 230 Bde, 20 O.R, 231 Bde, 40 O.R's 46 D.A.C.	
			2nd Lt C. JACKSON from 1st army school of Gunnery	
	19		Lt N.W. BEESON & 2nd Lt T.W. HARPHAM att. to 230 Bde	
			2nd Lts J. LEE, C. JACKSON, J. L. REID att. 231 Bde. Remount party returned	
			from BOULOGNE. 2 Remount mules each to Sect 1 & SAA Sect 46 DAC	
	20		20 L.D horses from SAA Sect. distributed to Bdes, 11 Remount mules from Bdes	
			to S.A.A. Sect.	
	21		Routine	
	22		Routine	
	23		2nd Lt D.K. ABRAHAMS att. to 231 Bde R.F.A, 2nd Lt J.L. REID returned from	
			231 Bde R.F.A to S.A.A. Sect 46 D.A.C.	
	24		Routine	

WAR DIARY or INTELLIGENCE SUMMARY

Army Form C. 2118.

46. D.A.C.
March 1918

Vol 38

Place	Date	Hour	Summary of Events and Information	Remarks and references to Appendices
LUGY	1		Routine	
"	2		Routine	
"	3		SAA Sec 46 DAC move from CREPY to NEDON	
"	4		H.Q. & Sections I - II move from LUGY to AMETTES	
NEDON			SAA Section move from NEDON to AMETTES	
			also T.M. Dumps at BEUVRY	
			H.Q. & Sec II move from AMETTES to VENDIN-LES BETHUNE. Sec I remains	
AMETTES	5		at AMETTES	
VENDIN-LES	6		T.M. DUMP BEUVRY handed over to 55th DIV	
BETHUNE	7		2nd Lt E PORTIER returns from returning T.M. School, & is posted to No 6 T.M. Bty	
"	8		SAA Sec 46 DAC commenced bomb store at LE QUESNOY	
"	9		2/Lt D & nukes from Sec I to M.V.S. & nukes from H.Q. to M.V.S	
"			2nd Lt C JACKSON returns from Corps gas course	
"	10		LE QUESNOY DUMP Formed 31 Reinforcements received from DIV DEPOT BATT	
"			and distributed to Btes as follows 1. 2 OR. 230 Bde. 2 3 OR 231 Bde. 26 OR DAC	
"	11		2/Lt J.A. NASH transferred to 46 T.M. Bty & Junior SAA Sec	
"	12		2nd & 2/Lt J.A STRACHAN & J.L. REID from ENGLAND posted to SAA Section	
"	13		Routine	
"	14		2nd Lt C JACKSON to 1st Army School of Sanitation	

CONFIDENTIAL.

WAR DIARY.

46th: DIVISIONAL AMMUNITION COLUMN.

MARCH 1st: to MARCH 31st: 1918.

46 D.A.C. WAR DIARY or INTELLIGENCE SUMMARY

Army Form C. 2118.

Place	Date	Hour	Summary of Events and Information	Remarks and references to Appendices
LUSY	24		Rouvres. Capt W. Savory on leave to England (1 week)	
"	25		A Echelon moved. 9 G.S. wagons daily to collect supplies at 2.3.1. Batt.	
"	26		Capt W.T. Wood R.A.M.C. returned from leave to England.	
"	27		Remount Raft consisting of 8 O.R.s returned from Boulogne Hand H. Vaccines [ ]one [ ] and [ ] to Sect II	
"	28		During [ ] found much event [ ]pers [ ] bent on rest. Subject: School Training has been carried out by Officers, N.C.O.s + men. Gun Drill + laying. Musketry, Ranging, [ ] on Car tracks have been given to Officers + [ ] N.C.O.s by day + night. Lectures [ ] Indian Personnel arrived from Base during the week. Have been detailed to Sect I, II + C.A.A. Respraying + Remount among work [ ] but a good deal of the Health of Troops - good [ ] Supplies very best adequate Weather cold + [ ] during the week	

M. [signature]
[signature] R.C.A.
Comm. 46 D.A.C.

WAR DIARY or INTELLIGENCE SUMMARY

Army Form C. 2118.

26th D.A.C.
February 1918

Place	Date	Hour	Summary of Events and Information	Remarks and references to Appendices
LUCY	14		142 Reinforcement (INDIAN PERSONNEL) from Base.	
	15		INDIAN PERSONNEL distributed as follows :- 32 Sec I, 29 Sec II, 41 SAA Sec I, 32 Sec II. Remainder of Indian detail to 230 Bde. from D.A.C. posted to 232 A.F.A. Bde.	
	16		Training of INDIAN PERSONNEL commenced. 2 Shoeing Smiths transferred to 232 A.F.A. Bde.	
	17		1 L.D. — 1 Mule to M.V.S.	
	18		Indian Officers joined from Base reported as follows:-	
			Jet T.W. HARHAM to Sec I	
			" C. JACKSON to Sec II	
			" J. LEE to Sec II	
	19		Jet F. PORTER to 1st Army T.M. School for 6" T.M. Course	
	20		Jet H. PAYNE on 14 days leave to England.	
	21		23 Reinforcement from Ord Depot, Bd'V. for hill to Base.	
	22		1 Reinforcement arrived from Base & posted to D.A.C.	
	23		8 6 R's from SAA Sec to Boulogne for collar commd.	

WAR DIARY or INTELLIGENCE SUMMARY

Army Form C. 2118

MmCol D.A.C.
February 1918
Vol 37

Place	Date	Hour	Summary of Events and Information	Remarks and references to Appendices
GONNEHEM	1		Orders received from 11.D.A.C.	nil
	2		Lt Col J H Huston struck off strength (Sick). A.S. No. D/1911. ERA No. 23/55	nil
			1 O.R. to 25th D.A.	
	3		Routine	nil
	4		Sgt. J. SAA to & took march	nil
	5		Lt. Col. J H Huston, R.S.M. T O'Callahan, Sergt Bowshed. awarded BELGIAN Croix	nil
			de Guerre. Four weeks earl. for Personal records	
	6		ORA inspected aircraft from Butts of DAC	nil
	7		13 O.R.s reinforcements from Base 100 DAC Trench to 2nd Regt Batt	nil
	8		5 O.R. reinforcements from Base 100 DAC - 66.2% Received recon to Put das	nil
			NEDONCHELLE on 10th, LUGY-ORERY on 11th	
	9		2 mules to M.V.S	nil
FONTAINE LES HERMANS	10		M.L. 1st & 2nd Sections March to new billet at FONTAINE LES HERMANS, SAA Section	nil
			Proceed to NEDONCHELLE	
LUGY	11		M.L. 1st - Sections march to LUGY. S.A.A Sect marched to ORERY	nil
	12		Rigor J. R. allow from 'DAC' goes to 48th DAC vacated Command	nil
			SAA Sect Supply 10 wagon daily to 130 Bde sup H.A.S. planting w/ 4.5 RA v 7 M's	
			& Solderr Armantz 3 G.S wagons daily to land & Echelon Brigs, SAA sect 3" G Waggons	
	13		daily to SAA Sel allotus 2 L.D.R 30 mules Ramory Park Boulogne to D.A.C	nil
			Reinforcement from Base: Captain B Mudget 2nd in Conr	

CONFIDENTIAL.

10

WAR DIARY.

46th: DIVISIONAL AMMUNITION COLUMN.

FEBRUARY 1st: to FEBRUARY 28th: 1918.

xxxxxxxxx

WAR DIARY
INTELLIGENCE SUMMARY

Place	Date	Hour	Summary of Events and Information	Remarks and references to Appendices
GONNEHEM	January 26		H.Q. & Section II marched to New Billets at GONNEHEM. No. 1 to VERDIN leaving our billets vacated by 11 o'clock. Route taken was Section I Hers & GONNEHEM – SAA Section – VERDIN & Train arrived & cleaning up a/c. Capt W.T. Long BRAE month leave	
—	27		Capt J.B. Murphy 14 day leave of absence to England.	
—	28			
—	29		1 Pun. to N.O.S.	
—	30		16 O.R. Reinforcements from L.W. Depot join — P.O.R. 23.0. & 30th 27 Pk. Training continued as	
—	31		The R.F.C. have moved into new billets during the latter part of month. The messes was satisfactory & the Modified scale of ration has been in operation from 17th & so far there has been no complaints. Performances of both officers & O.R's have been received during the month & were quite good. Officers require more instruction in Reconnaissance Reports have been received & more instruction on the animals. Messes among Officers & Sirdars has been very good during the month. Health of personnel has been very good during January Contr Senders etc issued for month of January	

46th F.A. Army Form C. 2118.
January 1918

WAR DIARY or INTELLIGENCE SUMMARY.

(Erase heading not required.)

Place	Date	Hour	Summary of Events and Information	Remarks and references to Appendices
VERQUIGNEUL	January 13		Lieut T.H. Wadding from 14 days leave of absence to England. 2/Lieut C.B. Burgess ADZ Thompson attached to 230 Bde for instruction. 2/Lieut T.P. Bramble & 33 ord attached for instruction. W.S.	
"	14		Horses received from BOULOGNE. 1 Riding + 12 mules W.S.	
"	15		1 L.D. + 8 mules from M.V.S. Modified issue of rations received from A/ccom W.S.	
"	16		2/Lieut A.W. Mulholland to R.F.C. from England W.S.	
"	17		Horses admitted to M.V.S.	
"	17		1 mule from M.V.S. 3 mules admitted to M.V.S.	
"			12 G.S. Wagons under 2/Lieut Mack. Lowder to E.O.B. UF DF C.B. U+S to work for his Train carrying rations from A/ccom to by Bde W.S.	
"	19		1 L.D. 1 Mule admitted to M.V.S.	
"	20		2/Lieut E.S. Luton from France to India & join 1 Poor HANDFHARS & his Regt proceed to India & join 1 Poor MANDFHARS & this unit W.S.	
"	21		2/Lieut E.G. Emerson to conducting Indian personnel to this unit W.S. for the purpose of moving blankets W.S.	
"	22		H.G.S. to Lapalty for moving blankets W.S.	
"	23		14 O.R.'s 6 G.S. 30 mules 2/Lieut Mack Indian unit withdrawn from MAZINGARBE & 14,12 G.S. under 2/Lieut Nash Indian unit withdrawn from MAZINGARBE W.S.	
"	24		Memorandum of ADM SAA section to GONNEHEM Reer details W.S.	
"	25		SAA Section move to New billets. Train a Lorrie Column W.S. all dumps of Mills Grenades + Trench Morters via Lt 11 M & W Lorrie Column W.S.	

WAR DIARY or INTELLIGENCE SUMMARY

Army Form C. 2118.

46th K.A.C. January 1918

Place	Date	Hour	Summary of Events and Information	Remarks and references to Appendices
VERQUISNIEUX	January 1		Lieut Col. Granston Hewat S.S. Lawson & 4 O.R's returned from advanced Indian cavalry depôt ROUEN when they have undergone a course in management of INDIAN personnel & Lieut Col T.H. Holton to ENGLAND on one months leave of absence - Capt W. Savory taken command of D.A.C. Lieut T.R.S. Arrowsmith takes over duties as Equipment officer admitted to M.V.S. from Sec II W.S	
—	2		PASTURE DUMP opened for supply of animals. 4 I.D. admitted to M.V.S. from Sec II W.S	
—	3		4 Mules & 1 I.D. admitted to M.V.S. Lieut G.G. Lawson 14 days.	
—	4		2 I.D. + 1 Mule from Sec I & 4 Mules from SAA the 4 M.V.S W.S	
—	5		Leave of absence to England W.S	
—	6		20 Reinforcements from D.A.C. oft 14 days at his before Rouen W.S	
—	7		1 I.D. from Sec I to M.V.S. W.S	
—	8		Lieut H. Spalding returned from leave W.S.	
—	9		Lieut F.W. Saunton 14 days leave of absence to England W.S	
—	10		2/Lieut T.A. NASH T.C. GILLESPIE & PORTER join D.A.C. reinforcement from England - 70 O.R.S & Bourgeon for Remounts W.S Officers Riding h. 147 hl. Been having been temporarily attached D.A.C. evacuated A.T.S.C.D. W.S	
—	11		Animals from Sec I tell cult, doubtful given to M.V.S. for slipping W.S Capt T.H. Humphries from leave having been 10 days extension from W.O. W.S	
—	12		4 Mules from SAA admitted to M.V.S. W.S	

CONFIDENTIAL.

WAR DIARY.

46th: DIVISIONAL AMMUNIYION COLUMN.

JANUARY 1st: to JANUARY 31st: 1918.

xxxxxxxxxxx

Vol 36

46 D.A.C.
WAR DIARY or INTELLIGENCE SUMMARY
Army Form C. 2118.

Place	Date	Hour	Summary of Events and Information	Remarks and references to Appendices
VERQUIGNEUL	29.12.17		2/Lt A.D.F. THOMPSON from Base to posted to A Section II. JWB	
	30.12.17		The following Officers joined 46 Div Arty on 26.12.17 & are posted to D.A.C. JWB	
			2/Lt W.R. BRADSHAW " W.H.J. HOOTEN " G.F. MORSE } attached to 230 Bde R.F.A. " E.F. HEAL	
			2/Lt H.J.N. BUTLER " S.W. BRIDGEWATER } attached to 231 Bde R.F.A. " S.A. JARDINE " A. ALEXANDER JWB	
	31.12.17		1 L.D. + 1 MULE returned to Vet. I from M.V.S. JWB	
			Ammunition delivered during the month:—	
			A 4x Bx BPS TMC Grenades 23 Broze V.P.A. Rockets S.A.A. 26,109 17,643 11891 200 207 3300 760 1272 130 1,846,000.	
			A large number of animals have been sent to M.V.S. for treatment of OPTHALMIA. Some of them are being returned cured.	
			The weather during the month has been dry & cold with some more shells of Anthrax pox good. Rations & forage good both in quality & amount. Discipline good.	
			JWB	

[Signature] W.C.I.R.P.A.
Comndg 46 D.A.C.

46 S.N.C.

Army Form C. 2118.

WAR DIARY
or
INTELLIGENCE SUMMARY.
(Erase heading not required.)

Instructions regarding War Diaries and Intelligence Summaries are contained in F. S. Regs., Part II. and the Staff Manual respectively. Title pages will be prepared in manuscript.

Place	Date	Hour	Summary of Events and Information	Remarks and references to Appendices
VERQUIGNEUL	12.xi.17		Lt H J SPALDING returns to duty from I Corps Musketry School. JHH	
	13.xi.17		Lt R S ARROWSMITH to ENGLAND for 14 days leave. 12 O.Rs returns from conducting remounts from BOULOGNE. 1 Rider Remount to Vet " II. JHH	
	14.xi.17		7 mules & I.L.D. to M.V.S. - Pittalunia. 1 Mule to M.V.S. JHH	
	15.xi.17		8 mules & I.L.D. to M.V.S. suffering from Pittalunia JHH	
	16.xi.17		11 O.Rs reinforcements from 51st Depot Battalion arrive. 3 Mules R.H.V.S. for Pittalunia. JHH	
	17.xi.17		Capt J H THURSFIELD to ENGLAND on 14 days leave. JHH	
	18.xi.17		4 mules to M.V.S. DROVIN for treatment of Pittalunia JHH	
	19.xi.17		1 O.R. Reinforcement from Vet Depot Battalion posted to Sect T. D.A.D.V.S. lectures on farriery all horses in D.A.C. JHH	
	20.xi.17		Routine JHH	
	21.xi.17		24 ORs to BOULOGNE to convey Remounts. JHH	
	22.xi.17		Capt J B MURPHY attends lectures at MERVILLE on Strategic Geography. JHH	
	23.xi.17		2 I.D. horses & 7 mules from M.V.S. returned to Sections. No 820273 Gr GASKIN WH from No 3 Military Prison HAVRE in unison on Sentence JHH	
	24.xi.17		Men of advanced SAA Section MAZINGARBE held Xmas Dinner JHH	
	25.xi.17		1 Mule returned to Sect III from M.V.S. 2/Lt NA BRAHWELL joins from Base & is posted to Sect II. JHH	
	26.xi.17		4/Lt C P BURGESS joins from Base & is posted to Sect I. Remounts arrive from BOULOGNE were distributed to Brigade. JHH	
	27.xi.17		49 Mules to D.A.C. JHH	
			1 Mule R.H.V.S. from Sect II JHH	
	28.xi.17		3 Mules I.L.D. & M.V.S. from SAA Section. I.L.D. R.H.V.S from Sect I. 2/Lt BRAHWELL to forward Bomb Store MAZINGARBE	
	29.xi.17		Lt N W BEESON to ENGLAND for 14 days Leave. Lt R S ARROWSMITH returns from leave to ENGLAND. JHH	

Army Form C. 2118.

WAR DIARY
or
~~INTELLIGENCE SUMMARY~~
(Erase heading not required.)

46th D.A.C.

Instructions regarding War Diaries and Intelligence Summaries are contained in F.S. Regs., Part II. and the Staff Manual respectively. Title pages will be prepared in manuscript.

Place	Date	Hour	Summary of Events and Information	Remarks and references to Appendices
VERQUIGNEUL	22.11.17		2/Lt. C.F. OLDRIDGE from 2/46 T.M. Bty for duty.	
	23.11.17		Lt. R.F. ARROWSMITH detached to 46 Div Depôt Battn for duty in charge of R.A. Personnel. F.G.C.M. on No 820758 Gunner SOUTHALL at SAILLY LABOURSE.	F.G.C.M. on No 820758
	24.11.17		36 ORs to No 7 Rifle Range for Musketry Practice. 5 ORs from Div Dep Battn posted to sect II. Promulgation of sentence of F.G.C.M. on No 820750 Gunner SOUTHALL - 42 days F.P. No I. 2/Lt MITCHELL G. returns from 14 days leave to ENGLAND.	2/Lt MITCHELL G. 42 days F.P. No I.
	25.11.17		2. Officers - 1.W.O. + 3 NCOs proceed to ROUEN to learn colloquial URDU + customs of NATIVE INDIAN drivers	
	26.11.17		2 Riders arrived from H.Q. R.A.	
	27.11.17		1 Remount Rider received & posted to sect II.	
	28.11.17		ALLAN DUMP handed over to 11 Divn. Lt WADDINGHAM returns to D.A.C. + is posted to sect II.	
	29.11.17		Section Inspection Field Service Marching Order by G.O.C. 46 Divn. 13 reinforcements ammon from Div Depôt Battn. - 1 & 23/Bde R.F.A - 12 posted to sections D.A.C.	
	30.11.17		2/Lt G. MITCHELL attached to 230 Bde R.F.A. 2/Lt. C.F. OLDRIDGE attached to 231 Brigade R.F.A. During the month the following ammunition has been received:- A. 29690 - A.X 3228.7. B.X. 16246. N. 4912. N.X 3930. T.M.G 200. T.M.F. 20. T.M.C. 2/21. Grenades No 5 48. No 28. 912. Rockets 231. S.A.A. 814.000 Flares 40 VPA 2994. Reinforcements received during the month have been of good standard. Remounts have been poor. Rations have been very good - Forage good - Heavy oil cake have been drawn. Health & Forage excellent - Discipline good.	

J.N. Hinton Lt Col RFA
O/c 46 D.A.C.

Army Form C. 2118.

WAR DIARY
or
INTELLIGENCE SUMMARY.
(Erase heading not required)

46th D.A.C.

Place	Date	Hour	Summary of Events and Information	Remarks and references to Appendices
VERQUIGNEUL	1.11.17		1 Officer + 7 ORs A.D.C. from I Corps Depot, attached to ALLAN DUMP for purpose of examining salved ammunition.	
	2.11.17		All 18 Pr Smoke Shell (1070 Rounds) returned to O.Y.C. from VERQUIGNEUL + ALLAN DUMPS. 1 Surplus Fitter + Surplus Wheeler sent to 285 + 295 Brigades R.F.A. respectively for duty. Authority R.A. Section 3rd Echelon.	
	3.11.17		New Standings erected for Animals of HQrs 46 D.A.C.	
	4.11.17		Farriers Leggett + others attached from 231 Bde R.F.A.	
	5.11.17		F.G.C.M. on No. 181478 Driver Pryke A. at SAILLY LABOURSE at 2 p.m.	
	6.11.17		Lt. E.N. SNOOK attached to Z/46 T.M. Bty - Capt. Thurefeld returned to duty from 230 Bde R.F.A.	
	7.11.17		1304 Rounds defective ammunition A + N returned in G.S. Wagons to O.M. VERQUIN from ALLAN DUMP.	
	8.11.17		5,500 Rds. B.X. Delivered to GARDEN DUMP from ALLAN DUMP by Light Car?	
	9.11.17		24 Remounts arrived from Remount Stage MARLES-LES-MINES. 20 distributed to Bdes R.F.A. 4 to M.V.S. Section I collar 2 Mules from 46 Signal Co. Section II 1 LD from 46 Sig.real Co. taken on strength B D.A.C.	
	10.11.17		1 Officer - 1 AVC Sergt - 1 Shoeing Smith + 3 ORs to BOULOGNE for Remounts. 1 Mare selected by I Corps Selection Committee at CHATEAU des PRES for breeding purposes.	
	11.11.17		2 Wagons G.S. + 2 Dial Sight No. 7 issued to 277 Bde R.F.A.	
	12.11.17		5 Horses each from Sect I + II sent to I Corps M. Vety. Detachments DROUVIN suffering from Malaria.	
	13.11.17		14 Reinforcements arrive from Base. 30 ORs to No. 14 Rifle Range for Musketry Practice	
	14.11.17		96 O.Rs. Musketry Practice at No. 14 Rifle Range. 14 Reinforcements sent to Divisional Depot Bn H r	
	15.11.17		2 Wagons G.S. sent to Brigades R.F.A.	
	18.11.17		48 ORs Musketry Practice at No. 7 Rifle Range	
	19.11.17		43 Drivers from 11 D.A.C. posted to 46 D.A.C.	
	20.11.17		43 Drivers from 11 D.A.C. to 46 Div Depot Bn Hr Capt J.B. MURPHY returns to duty from H.Q.R.A.	
	21.11.17		48 O.Rs from SAA Sect to No. 7 Rifle Range for Musketry Practice. 2/Lt J.H. RUDDOCK posted from 231 Bde R.F.A. to 46 D.A.C. + remains attached to X/46 T.M. Battery. Capt H. PAYNE returns from 3 P. Stays Leave to ENGLAND.	

CONFIDENTIAL.

WAR DIARY.

46th: DIVISIONAL AMMUNITION COLUMN.

NOVEMBER 1st: to NOVEMBER 30th: 1917.

****

Army Form C. 2118.

WAR DIARY
or
INTELLIGENCE SUMMARY.
(Erase heading not required.)

Instructions regarding War Diaries and Intelligence Summaries are contained in F. S. Regs., Part II. and the Staff Manual respectively. Title pages will be prepared in manuscript.

Place	Date	Hour	Summary of Events and Information	Remarks and references to Appendices
VERQUIGNEUL			A Salvage Dump has been formed in D.A.A Section lines. The Dumps at VERQUIGNEUL has been rebuilt + a new roof of Corrugated Iron put on. 1936 rounds B.X have been fired with 10 6 prize + issued to Batteries. A corresponding number of 18 pr, 20 has been returned to O.M. During the month training has taken place in the following. Driving Drill - Riding Drill - Musketry Practices - Arms + R/A Drill. Lectures Marching Orders and in N.C.O. + Lectures for N.E. O's. Animals have been clipped + need high. Much work has been done on building Horse standings + Billets + Drainage. Windscreens have been erected with Duck ties. 2 lbs of straw per day has been drawn for animals & given as chaff. A small quantity of Linseed Cake has also been drawn. Field Service Boots have been drawn for mounted men + also Warm Clothing. Ration Forage has been good. Reinforcements have been of good stamp. Remounts fair very good. Health of the troops excellent.	

J. Hinton Capt R.F.A
p. 46 D.A.C.

Army Form C. 2118.

WAR DIARY
or
INTELLIGENCE SUMMARY.
(Erase heading not required.)

Instructions regarding War Diaries and Intelligence Summaries are contained in F. S. Regs., Part II. and the Staff Manual respectively. Title pages will be prepared in manuscript.

Place	Date	Hour	Summary of Events and Information	Remarks and references to Appendices
VERQUIGNEUL	27.10.17		2/Lt R.D. CAMPBELL from 281 Bde RFA. 2/Lt R.D. CAMPBELL to hospital. 2/Lt R.J. HARNAH. 2/Lt E. ALLEN. 2/Lt E.A. HILLYARD. 2/Lt H.M. CLARKE. 2/Lt A.L. DAWSON join from 1/st ARMY Artillery School.	
	28.10.17		2 O.R. Reinforcements from Base. 2/Lt G.G. DAWSON returns from 1 Corps Musketry School. Lieut. H.S. HALL from 1st Army Artillery School. 2/Lt G. MITCHELL is post to 46 DAC (Part I) from 14th A.F.A. Bde – on appointment to Commission from B.S.M.	
	29.10.17		Lieut A.L. DAWSON. 2/Lt E. ALLEN. 2/Lt E.A. HILLYARD attached to 230 Bde RFA for duty. Lieut R.J. HARNAH. Lt. H.S. HALL + 2/Lt H.M. CLARKE attached to 231 Bde RFA for duty. 2/Lt F. EATON joins from 4th Army Artillery School.	
	30.10.17		2/Lt F. EATON attached to 230 Bde RFA for duty. 7 N.C.Os + 13 men to 1st Army French Mortar School.	
	31.10.17		17 Remounts collected from Remount Staging Camp L'EMONTE EVENTE issued to Brigades R.F.A.	
			During the noon ttt the following ammunition has been issued to Artillery + Infantry Brigades A.12328 – AX 19,954. A. Smoke 798 – B.X. 9206. B.P.S. 226. B.C.B.R. 300 B.V.N 300 N 4624. J.A.A. 4,162,000 Grenades No 22 – 1776 – No 24 – 60. No 5 – 2000. Grenades M.S.K. 34. Flares 115 Rockets 272. V.P.A. 150. T.M.B. 100. T.M.C. 4,632. Ring charges 3,100. The following ammunition has been collected from divisional Battery Positions + returned to ALLAN DUMP. A. 11.271. A.X. 5837. B.X. 2,169. N. 2460. N.X. 7650. This ammunition has been cleaned + boxed. DUNLOP DUMP has been cleared of all Ammunition + 30,000 empty boxes has been returned to O.M. VERQUIGNEUL.	

WAR DIARY
~~INTELLIGENCE SUMMARY.~~
(Erase heading not required.)

Army Form C. 2118.

Place	Date	Hour	Summary of Events and Information	Remarks and references to Appendices
VERQUIGNEUL	3/10/17		Capt J.B. Murphy returned from leave to ENGLAND.	
	4/10/17		One O.R. wounded delivering ammunition on Light Railway.	
	5.10.17		Capt J.B. Murphy proceeds to H.Q. 46 Div Arty as Learner to Staff Captain R.A.	
	6.10.17		Lt J.H. Waddingham proceeds to ALLAN DUMP (BULLY GRENAY) to take over from 60 D.A.C.	
	7.10.17		R.S.M. Nicholson + 31 O.Rs proceed to ALLAN DUMP. 10 O.Rs to Divisional Signalling School.	
	8.10.17		2/Lt A.W. Hillholland proceeds to G.H. Gis Army for duty. Capt W. Savory proceeds on leave to ENGLAND. 10 ORs. proceed to BOULOGNE for Remounts. 2/Lt G.G. Dawson from 230 Bde for duty.	
			2/Lt P.R. Wood attached 230 Bde for duty.	
	9.10.17		1 Rider - 1 Light Draught + 5 Mules drawn from 46 Div Train.	
	10.10.17		7 Remounts received from 6 D.A.C.	
	12.10.17		Capt W.T. Wood R.A.M.C. returns from leave. 2/Lt E.M. Snook returns from Veterinary course ABBEVILLE.	
	13.10.17		11 O.Rs. Reinforcements arrive - 3 distributed to Brigades. Premier-	
	14.10.19		10 O.Rs return with remounts from BOULOGNE. Remounts distributed. 14 obtained with D.A.C.	
			2/Lt G.G. Dawson proceeds to I corps Musketry School also 1.O.R.	
	17.10.17		2/Lt J.S. Alport + 2/Lt R.L.S. White posted to 251 B de R.F.A.	
	19.10.17		8 horses to 1/1 N & Mid Mobile Veterinary Section suffering from Pottalunia	
	20.10.17		4 N.C.Os proceed to 1st Div Depot Battalion on Smartening up course. 8 NCOs from Bde RFA+	
			5 NCOs from D.A.C. rejoin from Div Depot Battalion for a Rough Riders course.	
			Capt H. Payne proceeds on one month's leave to ENGLAND.	

CONFIDENTIAL.

WAR DIARY.

40th: DIVISIONAL AMMUNITION COLUMN.

OCTOBER 1st: to OCTOBER 31st: 1917.

Army Form C. 2118.

WAR DIARY
or
INTELLIGENCE SUMMARY.

(Erase heading not required.)

Instructions regarding War Diaries and Intelligence Summaries are contained in F. S. Regs., Part II. and the Staff Manual respectively. Title pages will be prepared in manuscript.

A.6.D.A.C.

Place	Date	Hour	Summary of Events and Information	Remarks and references to Appendices
			Green clover has been purchased locally, and clover has been cut in annum als. Supplies received during the month have been adequate. Transport has been good. Health of troops very good. Weather conditions during month have been excellent.	

October 1st 1917.

J.P. Kirkor
Lt. Col. R.A.
Commdg. 46 D.A.C.

WAR DIARY or INTELLIGENCE SUMMARY

Army Form C. 2118.

A6 D.A.C.

Summary of Events and Information

The following gun ammunition has been supplied to Batteries during the month:—

A	A.X.	B.X.	'A' Smoke	B.S.K.
6726 Rnds.	1034 Rnds.	6274 Rnds.	606 Rnds.	404

The following has been raised from forward dumps during the month:—

S.A.A.	3" T.M.C.	Gren No. 23	Gren No. 5	V.P.A.
1,500,000	5386	3168	1224	700

Rockets	T.M.F.	T.M.B.
300	50	300

1. Horses has been issued to Mange during the month.

Great progress has been made on Horse Standings during the month, drains have been made, and covering constructed. N.C.O's have received many drill and bayonet exercises. N.C.O's have finished each afternoon during the month to instruction.

The reinforcements arriving during the month have been of poor stamp.

Army Form C. 2118.

WAR DIARY
or
INTELLIGENCE SUMMARY.
(Erase heading not required.)

Instructions regarding War Diaries and Intelligence Summaries are contained in F. S. Regs., Part II. and the Staff Manual respectively. Title pages will be prepared in manuscript.

Place	Date	Hour	Summary of Events and Information	Remarks and references to Appendices
VERQUIN EQL	21/9/16		Promulgation of Fwd. General Court Martial on No. 820016 Sgt. F.R. White (Sect. HQ. AA.) Sentence of Court. Reduced to Corporal.	
	22/9/16		Lieut. E.S. Williams returns to "B" A. Col. from I.E.S. Army Artillery School. Promulgation of Field General Court Martial on No. 820,347 Gunner Ph. (Sect HQ. AA.) Sentence of Court. 6 months Imprisonment with Hard Labour.	
	23/9/16		Lieut. E.S. Williams posted to 231 Bde. R.F.A. 46th Divl. Reinforcements arrive from Base Depôt.	
	24/9/16		distributed to Batteries. "Societé of Maires" Committee of Breeding Inspec visit HQA. "B" A. Col. and inspect mares.	
	25/9/16		32 Reinforcements arrive from HQA. Divl. Depot Battn. and distributed to Brigades.	
	26/9/16		18 G.S. wagons and 1 Maltese Cart. Surplus to numbers. Sent for return to D.A.D.O.S. 46th DIVISION.	
	20/9/16		1 Officer and 2 Sgts. Proceed on VETERINARY COURSE at ABBEVILLE.	

WAR DIARY
or
INTELLIGENCE SUMMARY.
(Erase heading not required.)

Army Form C. 2118.

Place	Date	Hour	Summary of Events and Information	Remarks and references to Appendices
VERQUINEUL	11/9/17		12 Reinforcements arrive from Base and sent to Mul. Depot R.A. for training.	
"	12/9/17		2/Lt. E.F. Hollis to Trench Mortars from 46 A. Col. 2/Lt. J.H. Haddingham from Trench Mortars to 46 D.A. Col.	
"	16/9/17		2/Lt I.A. Pepper transferred to 46th Div. Artillery.	
"	17/9/17		20 O.R.s (reinforcements) arrive from 46 Div. Depot Bat. and distributed as follows. 10 O.R.s to 230 Bde R.F.A. 9 O.R. to 231 Bde R.F.A. 1 O.R. to 46 D.Am Col. A/Lt L.H.Hunter R.F.A. when on leave to England, and assumes command of 46" D. Am Col.	
"	19/9/17		Lieut on Officer attached to Brigades for instruction in Brigades.	
"	20/9/17		The following 2/Lt R.D. Campbell R.F.A. to 231 Bde R.F.A. " G.E. Dawson R.FA to 230 Bde R.F.A. The following officers return to 46 D.A.Col from Brigades, 2/Lt h.h Beeson R.F.A from 230 Bde R.F.A. " " h.R.Q.R. " 230 Bde R.F.A.	

Army Form C. 2118.

WAR DIARY
or
INTELLIGENCE SUMMARY

(Erase heading not required.)

Title: 46th D.A.C.

Place	Date	Hour	Summary of Events and Information	Remarks and references to Appendices
VECQUINEUL	2/9/17		The following amounts transferred to Brigades - Surpluses under establishment. 142 L.D. to 231 Bde. 41 L.D. to 230 Bde.	
"	7/9/17		Lieut. Col. H. Hudson R.F.A. Commanding "6" D.A.C. proceeds on leave to England. Command handed over to Captn. J. Swan R.F.A.	
			3. S. Gr. 4th D.A. Col. severely wounded whilst delivering ammunition.	
			MALINGARBE. 16 drivers by parking dump.	
			2 O.R. 4th D.A. Col. Killed, whilst with 2nd Canadian Tunnelling Cy.	
"	8/9/17		2/Lt. A.J. Wade R.F.A. 46th D.A. Col. admitted to Hospital. The following Officers attached to Brigades for instructional purposes.	
			2/Lt. H. Thrupp R.F.A. to 230. Bde. R.F.A. Lieut. B.A. Camp R.F.A. to 231. Bde. R.F.A.	
			The following Officers rejoin the D.A. Col. from attachment to Brigades.	
			2/Lt. E.L. Smart R.F.A. from 230 Bde. R.F.A.	
			2/Lt. E.L. Hollis R.F.A. " 231 " "	
"	14/9/17		23 Reinforcement arrivals from "6" Bde Training Depot and distributed to Brigades.	
			4 Reinforcements arrive from Base, and sent to 16" Divl. Training Depot.	

Army Form C. 2118.

WAR DIARY
or
INTELLIGENCE SUMMARY

(Erase heading not required.)

46. D.A.C.

Instructions regarding War Diaries and Intelligence Summaries are contained in F. S. Regs., Part II. and the Staff Manual respectively. Title pages will be prepared in manuscript.

Place	Date	Hour	Summary of Events and Information	Remarks and references to Appendices
HOUCHIN.	2/9/16		Adv. A.A.Col. move to new Area. Headquarter Staff, Sections 1 & 2, from HOUCHIN to VERQUINEUL.	
VERQUINEUL	"		B. Echelon from HOUCHIN to F20 Central. (REF MAP. SHEET 36 B/1/40,000) Advanced thing (Contrigeme S.A.A. Grenades, T.M.B, t.T.M.C.) taken over in toto by Div. Am. Col. at MAZINGARBE.	
F20 CENT.	"		Ammn dump. (Contrinue S.A.A. Grenades, T.M.B, t.T.M.C.) taken over by "B" Echelon 46. Div. Am. Col. of F20. CENT.	
VERQUINEUL	"		Ammn dump (comprising 4 for B.A.Col. Hom. 18 pdr, 4.5") taken over by 46R. B.A.Col from Br.A.Col. Hor. B.A.Col sent 30 O.R.s to 2nd. Australian Tunnelling Coy for work on heavy Trench Mortar dug-outs.	
"	3/9/16		Lieut. H. F. Reading joins 46R. B.A.Col. from 1st Army Artillery School.	
"	4/9/16		Field General Cont Martial held on No. 220, 347. Gnr Avon W. (See 40.A.A)	
"	5/9/17		Organisation of "46" B.A.Col. commenced view War Estab. Part VII.A. 4/8/917.	
"	6/9/17		In following our various surplus conveyance to the New Estab came but into true. 71.0 Rs. 155 Animals. 16 Wagons. O.S. 1 Mallette Cart. Change in designation "B" Echelon becomes S.A.A. Section	

CONFIDENTIAL.

WAR DIARY.

46th: DIVISIONAL AMMUNITION COLUMN

SEPTEMBER 1st: to SEPTEMBER 30th: 1917.

Army Form C. 2118.

46th D.A.C.

WAR DIARY
or
INTELLIGENCE SUMMARY.
(Erase heading not required.)

Place	Date	Hour	Summary of Events and Information	Remarks and references to Appendices
			Reinforcements arriving during month have been of good physique and good stamp generally. Remounts arriving during the month have been of fair stamp. Rations received during month have been good. Health of horses very good. Weather conditions during month, very inclement, rain, thunderstorms.	

J.F. Kirkton
Lt. Col. R.F.A.
Comm'ding 46 D.A.C.

Army Form C. 2118.

46th D.A.C.

WAR DIARY
or
INTELLIGENCE SUMMARY.
(Erase heading not required.)

Place	Date	Hour	Summary of Events and Information	Remarks and references to Appendices
HOUCHIN	26/8/17		2 Lt. N.F. Waide from 230 Bde R.F.A. and 2 Lt. D.A. Col. 19 reinforcements drawn from NOEUX-LES-MINES Railhead. "B" Echelon 46th D.A. Col. rationed by 1st Division. Major Beatty from 46th Divl Am. Sub. Col transferred to T.M. Battery. I. O. R's.	
	27/8/17			
	29/8/17		There is nothing special to report during the month. Ammunition has been drawn and G.S. wagons from advanced dump and delivered to gun positions. Musketry practice has been carried out by N.C.O's and men at Capt. Muckety's range. Roughly 4 & 8. ORA base fired. Much work has been done during the month on Horse. Standings, which are now in very good condition. Two T.M. Gunners have received instruction, Trench Mortar Gun drill. On 1st August the oat ration was reduced from 11lbs to 12 ozs. on account of the inclement weather experienced. Green clover has been purchased locally, also oaten hay has been cut for animals. During the month grazing has been ground for all animals in exchange for manure.	

Army Form C. 2118.

WAR DIARY
INTELLIGENCE SUMMARY. 46th D.A.C.
(Erase heading not required.)

Instructions regarding War Diaries and Intelligence Summaries are contained in F. S. Regs., Part II. and the Staff Manual respectively. Title pages will be prepared in manuscript.

Place	Date	Hour	Summary of Events and Information	Remarks and references to Appendices
HOUCHIN.	18/8/17		1. O.R. Killed. 1 O.R. wounded and 5 mules killed whilst conveying amn. to b/230. position. 13. O.Rs. m. 13. Transn. orter personnel. H6. R.S.M. & H6. D.A.Col. exchange. 13. O.Rs. transn. mtrs. personnel. 2/Lt.R.S.H. whilst from leave to England. 2/Lt.D.A.Col. exchange. 1. O.Rs. Du. Am.Col. to 2.31. Bde. R.F.A. for duty.	
"	19/8/17		2/Lt.R.S.H. Ikh.Rs. from nominal. Du. Am.Col. to 2.31. Bde. R.F.A. for duty.	
"	20/8/17		2/Lt.R.S.H. Ikh.Rs. from nominal. Field General Court Martial held on no. 820. 347. Gnr. Moor.N. Section 3. H6. D.A.Col. (Sect.n. H6. A.A.)	
"	21/8/17		2/Lt.G.Dawson from leave to England. V.46.T.M.Battery attached to H6. D.A.Col. for 1 week, for duty. Promulgation of Field General C.M. action on Gnr. Moor. N. Sentence - 6 months Imprisonment Hard Labour. Punishment No. 1. Remitted to 90 days. Commanding H6. Dn. Am.Col. takes over. Lt. Col. J. H. Hurton Commanding of H6. Dvl. Artillery.	
"	25/8/17		Lt. Col. S. Williams returns from Corps. dump. and proceeds to Army Artillery School.	
"	26/8/17		2/Lt.C.L. Okinclass taken over Corps. dump. HERSIN. 3 H6. Section 46 D.A.C. transferred to 6ty.ty. 15th Divn. 1. Officer. 3. R.Cos. and 114. O.Rs. take over Gunner. S.A.A. dump. at MAROC. and LES BREBIS.	

A.5834 Wt.W4973/M687 750,000 8/16 D.D.& L. Ltd. Forms/C.2118/13

WAR DIARY or INTELLIGENCE SUMMARY

Army Form C. 2118.

46th D.A.C.

(Erase heading not required.)

Instructions regarding War Diaries and Intelligence Summaries are contained in F.S. Regs. Part II. and the Staff Manual respectively. Title pages will be prepared in manuscript.

Place	Date	Hour	Summary of Events and Information	Remarks and references to Appendices
HOUCHIN	2/8/17		2/Lt. H.W. Mulholland posted to Hd. D.A.C. from 230 Bde. R.F.A.	
"	4/8/17		17 reinforcements arrive from Base, and proceed to 46. D.A. Col.	
"	6/8/17		2 Lts. R.S. Arrowsmith from leave in England.	
"	9/8/17		2/Lt. G.G. Danton proceeds on leave to England. 2/Lt. E.S. Williams takes over Corps Ammn dump at HERSIN.	
"	10/8/17		Signalling School formed — 12 O.R's. from Hd. D.A. Col. and 6 O.R's. from Trench Mortars) and 1 Sgt. Signalling instructor (from Hd. D.A. Col.)	
"	12/8/17		1 Officer and 31 O.R's. proceed to Remounts Camp at CAUCHY - RIGOUART, drew 31 remounts (Hughs draughts). 22 distributed to Artillery Bdes. 9 Section 2, Hd. D.A. Col. reached Billets at FOSSE-DIX-DUPONT and move to HOUCHIN.	
"	13/8/17		Capt. A.G. Clayton, Barker proceeds on leave to England. 2/Lt. H.F. Haigh to B/230 Bty for duty.	
"	14/8/17		10 Reinforcements arrive from Base and distributed as follows :- 9 to 231 Bde. R.F.A. 1 " 46" Trench Mortar Battery.	

CONFIDENTIAL.

WAR DIARY.

46th: DIVISIONAL AMMUNITION COLUMN.

AUGUST 1st: to AUGUST 31st: 1917.

WAR DIARY
or
INTELLIGENCE SUMMARY.

Army Form C. 2118.

A6 DAC

Place	Date	Hour	Summary of Events and Information	Remarks and references to Appendices
			On 23rd July the oat ration was reduced from 12 lbs to 11 lbs. Green clover has been purchased locally, also clover hay has been cut for animals. During the month grass up has been procured for all animals in exchange for rum ration. Reinforcements arriving during the month have been of good physique and good stamp generally. Remounts arriving during the month, have been of fair stamp. Rations received during month have been good. Health of troops very good. Weather, fine and warm, until the end of the month, when conditions very inclement, rain & thunderstorms.	

3/8/17.

J.H. Wilson
Lieut Col R.A.
Comdg A6th D.A.C.

WAR DIARY
INTELLIGENCE SUMMARY — A6 D.A.C.

Army Form C. 2118.

Place	Date	Hour	Summary of Events and Information	Remarks and references to Appendices
HOUDAIN	25/7/17		Promulgation of F.G.C.M. on No. 620, 243. Gnr Easton N.H. Sentence 6 months Imprisonment.	
"	27/7/17		1 O.R. wounded, and 3. L.D. wounded by enemy shell fire, whilst delivering Amn to gun positions, returns from BOULOGNE Capt. H. Payne and H1. O.R's return with remounts from 17. to D.A.Col. Corps Commander inspects no 1 D.A.Col.	
"	"		During the month the following Ammun was taken to Battery positions, and forward Infantry dumps.	

	A.	A.X.	B.X.	R.P.S.	T.M.F.	T.M.C.	T.M.B.	S.A.A.
	114,917.	8,162.	4,980	10	50	262	240.	540,000

No. S. Gdes.   No. 23 Gdes.
12,148.   456.

Much work has been done during the month on horse-standings, which are now in very good condition. Musketry instruction has been given every afternoon to N.C.O's & men also trained French Mortar personnel, have received instruction in T.M. gun drill.

WAR DIARY
INTELLIGENCE SUMMARY
(Erase heading not required.)

Army Form C. 2118.

A6 D.A.C.

Place	Date	Hour	Summary of Events and Information	Remarks and references to Appendices
HOUCHIN	14/7/17		Lt. E.S. Williams Lt. D.A.Can from 147' AFA Bde R.F.A. to 46' D.A.C. 1. Reinforcement from Base, + sent to 230 Bde R.F.A.	
"	19/7/17		2/Lt A.A. Blyfor transferred from 46' D.A.C. to 6" Divl. Arty. 2/Lt M.H. Graham and H.C. Coombs pozn to 230 Bde. from 46' D.A.C. Promulgation of ½ Cm on No. 820,099 Bom Hudson ½ S Sentence - Reduced to the rank of Gunner.	
"	19/7/17		64 Remounts received from BOULOGNE. 2/Lt N.F. Waite 46' D.A.C. on leave to England. Capt. A. Payne. 46' D.A.C. returned from leave to England.	
"	20/7/17		Ammunition dump BARLIN cleared of all Amm. boxes +C. 19. Reinforcements from Base. 15 to Brigades, + to D.A.C. ½ Cm on No. 820,243 Gnr. Parkin. W. High Staff 46' D.A.C. (Sect. 18 +(a) A.A.).	
"	21/7/17		Capt. H. Payne R.F.A. and 41. O.R's proceed to BOULOGNE to draw Remounts.	
"	22/7/17		Lenet. Morts. Camp, bombed by Hostile Aircraft. 2. O.R's killed. 6. O.R's wounded.	
"	24/7/17		No. 112,911 Gnr. Heal. B.S. Section 1. 46' D.A.C. attempted suicide. Cut throat.	

Army Form C. 2118.

WAR DIARY
or
INTELLIGENCE SUMMARY. 46 D.A.C.
(Erase heading not required.)

Place	Date	Hour	Summary of Events and Information	Remarks and references to Appendices
HOUCHIN.	6/7/17		9 Reinforcements arrive from Base. 2 O.R's to D/231. B/y, 1 to D.A.C. 12 O.R's from "46" D.A.C. to D/231 B/y to replace casualties.	
"	7/7/17		↑ E.Cm on No. 113911. Gm. Neal B. of "46" D.A.C. (Sect. B. (2 & 6) AA). Capt H. Payne. R.F.A. O.C. "B" Echelon "46" D.A.C. on leave to England. Capt W. Savery R.F.A. Arty. "46" D.A.C. returned from leave to England.	
"	8/7/17		2/Lt. F.A. Pepper from Base, posted to Sect. 2. "46" D.A.C.	
"	9/7/17		A.R.P. AIX. NOULETTE handed over by "46" D.A.C. to 2nd Canadian Divl. Am. Col. Anti-gas goggles recalled vide A.R.O. 1230 and handed over to Railhead for transmission to Base. Trench Mnts personnel "46" Divl. Arty to HOUCHIN. from BULLY-GRENAY.	
"	10/7/17		↑ E.Cm on no. 620.099. Bdr. Hudson L.J. "46" D.A.C. (Sect 19.A.A) Promulgation of F.G.Cm on no. 113911. Gm. Neal. B. of "46" D.A.C. Sentence 42 days F.P. NO.1.	
"	11/7/17		2/Lt. A. Blythe from 230 Bde. R.F.A. to "46" D.A. Col. 5. S.A.A. Carts received from Ordnance.	
"	12/7/17		14 new G.S. wagons and returned wagons to Base. Unserviceable wagons returned to Base.	

Army Form C. 2118.

WAR DIARY
INTELLIGENCE SUMMARY. 46 D.A.C.
(Erase heading not required.)

Place	Date	Hour	Summary of Events and Information	Remarks and references to Appendices
HOUCHIN.	1/4/17	—	G.S. Wagon of "A" & "B" sections +6" D.A.C. impressed for the purpose of condemning those found to be unserviceable. 2/Lt. E.H. Jobson returned from leave to England.	
LE BREBIS.	3/4/17		2/Lt. E.H. Gillam's section 2, +6" D.A.C., wounded, and 1 charger killed by enemy shell fire, whilst conveying ammun. to gun rock position. 2/Lt. C.F. Orridge to 1 +6. T.M. Btty. from +6" D.A. Col. under Canadian Corps. administration.	
HOUCHIN.	4/4/17		The following officers attached to Brigades for instructional purposes. 2/Lt. N.W. BEESON. } from +6" D.A.C. to 230 Bde R.FA " E.N. SNOOK. " R.W.T. JONES.	
"	5/4/17		2/Lt. E.H. ROYCE. " T.A. WOODHOUSE } from +6" D.A.C. to 231. Bde R. FA " W.E. RIDGEWAY " H. SPALDING 2/Lt. M.N. Graham. from 230 Bde R.FA to +6" D.A.C. 2/Lt. R.Sh. White " 231. Bde R. FA to +6" D.A.C.	

CONFIDENTIAL.

WAR DIARY.

46th: Divisional Ammunition Column.

JULY 1st: to JULY 31st: 1917.

Army Form C. 2118.

46th D.A.C.

WAR DIARY
or
INTELLIGENCE SUMMARY.
(Erase heading not required.)

Instructions regarding War Diaries and Intelligence Summaries are contained in F.S. Regs., Part II. and the Staff Manual respectively. Title pages will be prepared in manuscript.

Place	Date	Hour	Summary of Events and Information	Remarks and references to Appendices
HOUCHIN	27.6.17		1 Driver + 14 L.D. issued to Bdes. 5 Riders + 10 L.D. retained in D.A.C.	
	29.6.17		2/Lt H.C. COOMBS returned from 1st Army Sig. making School + reposted to Sect. II. 2/Lt A.W. BEESON returned from 1st Army Artillery School reposted to Sect. I.	
	30.6.17		During the month the following amounts of ammunition have been issued to Brigades R.F.A. + Infantry. A. 78,847. A.X. 49,461. B.X. 20,372. B.E.B.A. 2,184. B. Smoke 800. B.B.F. 726. A. Smoke 1472. T.M.B. 2,626. T.M.F. 700. S.A.A. 885,000. N°20 Grenades 230. N°24 Grenades 280. Flares 2000. Cart. pist. illum. meeting 1,820. Rockets 36. In addition Amm. unition has been collected from ARTESIAN sidings + delivered to 8 T.M. Batteries + advanced infantry Dumps. Also R.E. material to Batteries R.F.A. + T.M. Batteries. Green pads has been left in advanced areas + collected for horses. Some Grazing for horses has also been obtained. Remounts received have not been of good quality 7 on arrival have been sent M.V.S. for veterinary reasons. Reinforcements have been of good stamp. Rations good during month - Forage good - Health of troops excellent - discipline good.	

J.H. Kelso Lt Col. R.F.A.
O/c 46 D.A.C.

46th D.A.C.

Army Form C. 2118.

WAR DIARY
or
INTELLIGENCE SUMMARY.
(Erase heading not required.)

Instructions regarding War Diaries and Intelligence Summaries are contained in F. S. Regs., Part II. and the Staff Manual respectively. Title pages will be prepared in manuscript.

Place	Date	Hour	Summary of Events and Information	Remarks and references to Appendices
HOUCHIN	1.6.17		2/Lt Spalding returns from 1st Army Artillery School.	
	3.6.17		2/Lt HM Beeson to 1st Army Artillery School - 2/Lt R.S. Arrowsmith proceed to Musketry Course	
	5.6.17		Capt A.G. Clayton Barber joins 46 D.A.C. from 147 A.F.A. Brigade & posted to Sect II.	
	6.6.17		2Lt Waddingham & 2/Lt Roper E.L.R. arrive from Base.	
	8.6.17		2/Lt Walling Ham A.H. posted to 46th T.M.s. Capt R.F. Martin appointed Staff Captain R.A. dated 7/6/17.	
	13.6.17		Gunner Dalby welcomed from H.M. Military Prison Sir M. Field - under suspended Sentence Feb 1915. Sentence 2 years H.L. confirmed 1 year - posted to Sect. I. 46th Div Sports	
	14.6.17		2/Lt H.W. Cain & 2/Lt C.F. Oldridge attached to 230 B.& R.F.A/Division T.M. Cou. 2/Lt C.K. Hollis attached 231 B/ R.F.A. proceed to 1st Army T Mortar School	
	16.6.17		Promulgation of Court Martial on No. 108586 Dr Worthing Geo. W. sentenced to 90 days F.P. No 1. for Disobeying a lawful command. A.H. Sgt Sect 9 - 2	
	17.6.17		2/Lt Woodhouse T.H. joins from Base & posted to B Echelon.	
	18.6.17		to I Corps Schur.	
	20.6.17		2/Lt Spalling & 22 O.Rs. to BOULOGNE for Remounts. 26 Reinforcements arrive from Base.	
	22.6.17		26 Reinforcements distributed 13 to 230 Rf - 13 to 231 B.& Casualties owing to Shell fire in LIEVIN whilst delivering Grenades to Divis'l Infantry. Sniper. 2.O.Rs wounded - 1 horse killed 4 horses wounded. Capt. Wood. R.A.M.C. rejoins from leave to ENGLAND.	
	24.6.17		8 O.Rs. returned from 46 D.A. Signalling School. 12 O.Rs to 46 Div'l S.Y. Signalling School.	
	26.6.17		2/Lt Spalling H. & 22 ORs return from BOULOGNE with Remounts. 180 Remounts received & distributed to Units B. 6th & 46th Divisions. 2/Lt ARROWSMITH R.S. & 16 O.Rs. proceed to 1st GONNEHEM	
	27.6.17		2/Lt Arrowsmith - 16 O.Rs return from GONNEHEM with remounts. 6 Riders & 24 L.D.	

CONFIDENTIAL.

WAR DIARY.

46th: DIVISIONAL AMMUNITION COLUMN

JUNE 1st: to JUNE 30th: 1917.

WAR DIARY
or
INTELLIGENCE SUMMARY.
(Erase heading not required.)

Army Form C. 2118.

46 P.A.C.

Place	Date	Hour	Summary of Events and Information	Remarks and references to Appendices
	2/6/17		There is nothing special to report. The Services mean review. The Officers ionnig have had their usual Courses at Cadet Schools in England, but turn very little about Horsemanship. The Remounts received are good. The men from NOEUX. LES. MINES to HOUCHIN area are advantages, as in the former place, the men are very scattered, owing to being billetted in twos, threes in houses of the inhabitants. The present area is gone in every way. Forage and rations for the month have been adequate. Wherefore has been good. Capt R.J. Martin & Mr. J. Previas Section 3. have been mentioned in Officials despatches during the month.	

W Savery Lieut R.F.A.
O.C. 46: D.A. Col.

46th DAC

WAR DIARY
or
INTELLIGENCE SUMMARY.
(Erase heading not required.)

Army Form C. 2118.

Place	Date	Hour	Summary of Events and Information	Remarks and references to Appendices
HOUCHIN	26/5/17		1. Officer & 24 O.R's returned from BOULOGNE with remounts. B.A.C. advanced Ammn dump at AIX NOULETTE bombed by hostile aircraft about 10.30 p.m. 1. O.R. wounded.	
"	29/5/17		2. R.E. Orderlys sent to 230 Bde R.F.A. for instructional purposes. F.E.Cm. on No. 92054. Cpl. Scott F. Sect 6 (1 B) A.A.) F.E.Cm. on No. 820942 Dr. Smith S. " " (Sect F (2) A.A.)	
"	30/5/17		Promulgation of F.E.Cm. on 92054. Cpl. Scott F. (Reduced to Bombdr). " " " " 820442. Dr. Smith S. (56 days F.P.No.1) The following Ammn. has been issued to Batteries by G.S. wagons & lorries during the month.	
			A.X 32,900	A.X 16,236	B.X 10,968	R.C.R.R 1448	B.T.R.R 1062
			B.S.K 50		SMOKE SHELL 1832		T.M.F 340

WAR DIARY or INTELLIGENCE SUMMARY

Army Form C. 2118.

46 DAC

Place	Date	Hour	Summary of Events and Information	Remarks and references to Appendices
HOUCHIN.	8/5/17		Lieut C. Ralme. Section 2. No. 1 D.A.C. taken command of. X46. T.M. Battery. Major Caddock, & 2 of his horses + Graham gun B.A.C. from Base. 5 Remounts to Section 1. B.A.C. from Base. 5 " " 2 " " " 11 " " 3 " " "	
"	9.5.17.		Major Caddock. to 230 Bde. R.F.A. S.A.A. to move from dump at BARLIN. to forward dump.	
"	10.5.17		2/Lt. Hord. Graham to Headqr. 230 Bde R.F.A.] for instructional 2/Lt. Hollis + Hillis to Headqr 231 " "] purposes. 33 Reinforcements arrive from Base. + distributed to Brigades.	
"	12.5.17			
"	15.5.17		2/Lt. H. Spedding to 1st Army School. for course of instructors. 2/Lt. H. Cain. from School.	
"	16.5.17		2/Lt. N.H. Beam to B.A.C. from Base.	
"	19.5.17		2/Lt. E.M. Short, G.J. Oldridge, H.C. Coombs gun from T.M. Schl.	
"	21.5.17		1 Officer + 74 O.R. proceed to BOULOGNE to collect remounts.	
"	23.5.17		2/Lts. R.N. Oven + H.E. Ridgeway to B.A.C. from Base.	
"	25.5.17		HOUCHIN bombed by hostile aircraft about 10.30 p.m. 1. O.R. + 2 mules.	

46DAC

Army Form C. 2118.

WAR DIARY
INTELLIGENCE SUMMARY
(Erase heading not required.)

Instructions regarding War Diaries and Intelligence Summaries are contained in F.S. Regs., Part II. and the Staff Manual respectively. Title pages will be prepared in manuscript.

Place	Date	Hour	Summary of Events and Information	Remarks and references to Appendices
NOEUX-LES-MINES	1.5.17		2/Lt. L.H. Ruddock & 2/Lt. E.S.S. Ayer to 231 Brigade R.F.A.	
"	"		1 Officer + 23 O.R's proved by lorry to GONNEHEM to draw remounts to Riders. 30. R.D. Fr. D.A.C. & remainder distributed to Brigades. 2/Lt. H.H. Cain R.F.A. proceeds to 1st Army School for course of instruction.	
"	2.5.17		2/Lt. F.R.R. White from 1st Army School. 1 Officer + 34 O.R's proceed to BOULOGNE to draw remounts. 2/Lt. O.A. Hollis joins from Base. O.C. D.A.C. + Lieut. Bomb. Officer reconnoitre positions for advance. Grenade dump	
"	3.5.17		14. Reinforcement - join from Base. 15 to Brigades, 4 to D.A.C.	
"	4.5.17		6. O.R's wounded by shell fire, also 8 mules. 2/Lt. P.L. Swift + C.J. Oldridge H.C. Coomber proceed to Trench Mortar School for course of instruction. Sections 1 + 3 March from NOEUX-LES-MINES to new billets at HOUCHIN.	
"	"		2. O.R's wounded by shell fire, also 1 mule. Hdqr. A.S. Col. move to new billets at HOUCHIN. Section 2. remain at FOSSE-ALE-DUPONT.	

CONFIDENTIAL.

WAR DIARY.

46th: DIVISIONAL AMMUNITION COLUMN

MAY 1st: to MAY 31st: 1917.

/ 6th WAR DIARY D.A.C.
or
INTELLIGENCE SUMMARY.

Army Form C. 2118.

Place	Date	Hour	Summary of Events and Information	Remarks and references to Appendices
BRACQUEMONT	29/4/17		Part II dip all horses & mules at Munqs Dip BARLIN. 820400 Gr Pranley presented with Military Medal by G.O.C 46 th Div.	
	30/4/17		Part I & Echelon dip all horses & mules at Dip BARLIN. Reinforcements received during the month have been of good stamp. Officers sent for reinforcements have all had courses at ARTILLERY Schools in ENGLAND - staff have all served either in O.T.C. or infantry units in the FIELD. Remounts received were good. Health of the troops good - Discipline good. Billets in different areas occupied during the month have been good - men have had several opportunities for baths, horse lines until present area was reached were bad. Horses stood in field where cities were very muddy. Horses & mules are showing improvement since last month. Rations & supplies during the month have been good.	

J.P.Hinton / Lt / RFA(T)
OC 46 D.A.C.

A.6.* WAR DIARY D.A.C.
or INTELLIGENCE SUMMARY.

Army Form C. 2118.

Place	Date	Hour	Summary of Events and Information	Remarks and references to Appendices
L'ECLEME.	17/4/17		A. Echelon collect from Railhead ST VENANT 100 8000 rounds S.A.A.	
	18/4/17		2/Lt Dyer S.S. 2/Lt Durson G.G. 2/Lt Oldridge C.F. 2/Lt Morris G.S. arrive from Base, were posted to B.D.A.C.	
	19/4/17		150,000 Rounds S.A.A. Drawn from O.V. ST VENANT. by Sect II to complete.	
	20/4/17		2/Lt Cairn H.W from Base	
	22/4/17		Lieut. J. B. Murphy proceeds to SAINS-EN-GOHELLE to take over H.W Humshier Transport from 2/Lt Otts & was The following details supplied by B. Echelon. 2 Wagons G.S. H Teams w/m & pair Wheelers to Camp Commandant LA BUISSIERE. 1 Wagon S.S. F team w/m & pair Wheelers to 8th Labour Coy DRUVIN. 1 pr. Horses with harness to LAPUGNOY Railhead. 1 Wheeler & Town Major MAZINGARBE. 1 Wheeler & Town Major VERQUIGNEUL. B.H.D Horses to Corps Road Office at LA BUISSIERE. The following were sent to units for move to new area — 2 - Horse Teams to 230 & 231 Batteries. 1 Wagon G.S. & 4 G.T.M Batteries.	
	23/4/17		2/Lt Byer 1.N.C.O & 5 O.Rs proceed to 2nd D.A.C to take over Grenade Dump. 2/Lt Arrowsmith & 2/Lt Oldridge 1 N.C.O 1 Driver 3 gr. Veys 6 17 2 N.C.Os & 17 O.Rs proceed to SAINS EN GOHELLE to take over A.R.P from 24th Div.	
	24/4/17		D.A.C move to new area in the line Hd-Qrs & E-BECHELON to FOSSE dite de BRACQUEMONT. Sect II to FOSSE dite BECHELON to FOSSE dite la BRACQUEMONT. Sect II to FOSSE dite DUPONT. Delay of 2 hours in entering new billets was caused through unit being relieved not leaving area in good condition. but all horses in new area in good condition.	
FOSSE dite ar BRACQUEMONT.	27/4/17		2/Lt Morris G.S. posted to 280 B.C. — 2/Lt White - 2.N.Cos & 22 O.Rs. detached for purpose of taking in Ammunition. from old German gun positions. No 820400 Gun Hawley feet I awarded The Military Medal for pluck and grit when his horses were wounded. 2/Lt Spalding H. from Base.	
	28/4/17		2/Lt H.C. Coombs from Base. 40 O.Rs from Base 2 sent up to Brigades R.F.A. 2 posted to D.A.C.	

46th D.A.C. WAR DIARY

INTELLIGENCE SUMMARY

Army Form C. 2118.

Place	Date	Hour	Summary of Events and Information	Remarks and references to Appendices
ANVIN	1/4/17		A Echelon move to new Billets at FONTES. B Echelon move to MAZINGHEM.	
FONTES	2/4/17		D.A.C. Drivers & horses loaned to Brigades R.F.A. for march to New Area were returned to D.A.C. Remounts & driving marching until D.A.C. returned to their respective Batteries.	
	5/4/17		Full dismounted parade of D.A.C. & T.M. personnel in Chateau Grounds MAZINGHEM for distribution by G.O.C. 46th Div. of medal Ribbons. Sergt. T. Griffiths received Military Medal delivering S.A.A. & B/E2 W/OO under heavy fire showing marked courage & command under difficult circumstances. 7 Officers + 40 O.Rs arr. from Base. 4 Officers + 40 O.Rs sent to Brigades. Lieut Thursfield I/R - 24/T.M. Rudman - 2/Lt Campbell R.D. + 1 O.R. to D.A.C.	
	6/4/17		24 O.Rs from Base were distributed to Brigades.	
	9/4/17		Field Service Marching Order Parade of 46 Divn for Inspection by G.O.C. II Corps. On this occasion the Corps Commander & G.O.C. R.A. expressed themselves as very pleased with the D.A.C. During the stay in this AREA opportunity was taken to repaint all G.S. Wagons + S.A.A. Carts. Training was carried out which consisted of Gun Drill - Signalling - Marching Order Parades - Baking - Brigade Staff exercises for Officers, lectures on Horsemastership by V.O. Artillery subjects by O.C. A Divisional Staff ride was carried out under G.O.C. Division. O.C. D.A.C. attended as O.C. B/R.F.A.	
	13/4/17	5:45 a.m.	D.A.C. move to new Billeting Area. A Echelon to L'ECLEME - ROBECQ Road - B Echelon to BUSNES. 2 Wagons G.S. complete were sent to D.T.M.O. to assist T.M. Batteries to move. 5 wagons G.S. each sent to 230 + 231 B/100 R.F.A. + 4 wagons G.S. to HQ. R.A. to assist in move to new Area. Three wagons were called with D.A.C.	
L'ECLEME	14/4/17		2/Lt. SAHHAW.H. from Base reported to Unit. 2 Wagons G.S. loaned to 230 + 231 Bdes each to assist them in drawing Supplies. B Echelon draws from 1st ARMY Trnsp. LAPUGNOY 244 Ax. 72 S.A. 792 Bx.	
	15/4/17		16 O.Rs from Base & distributed to Brigades. 2/Lt. SAHHAW.H. posted to 230 Bde R.F.A. B Echelon sent 1 NCO + 11 drivers to THEROUANNE to draw 11 Limbered S.A.A. Carts for Infantry Brigades	

CONFIDENTIAL.

WAR DIARY.

46th: DIVISIONAL AMMUNITION COLUMN.

APRIL 1st: to APRIL 30th: 1917.

Army Form C. 2118.

WAR DIARY
or
INTELLIGENCE SUMMARY.

46 D.A.C.

(Erase heading not required.)

Place	Date	Hour	Summary of Events and Information	Remarks and references to Appendices
LE MEILLARD	30.3.17		A Echelon & French Mortars march to BOUBERS. B Echelon to MONCHEL.	
BOUBERS.	31.3.17		A Echelon & French Mortars march to GANVIN. B Echelon to TILLY CAPPELLE. During the march horses were watered en route. Water was obtained from pits. Two convoys on Vehicles. The first halt of the march & carrying of water was full of worn. B this means it was possible to water at advantageous places irrespective of whether water was available or not. It also insured the horses all drawing well. During the march there were casualties among the horses — 1 died — 1 wounded — 4 left behind for owners. Much ammunition during the march was delivered direct to gun positions. The Division moved forward & ammunition was delivered in G.S. Wagons for one night. As there was difficulty in getting wagons & this was discontinued & pack animals were used. Forward dumps were formed & supplied by G.S. Wagons. Pack animals were used from the dumps to gun positions. It was found more convenient for pack animals to carry ammunition both boxed & unboxed as was delivered in this way.
735 rounds A + 1151 AX were collected from unmanned gun positions returned to ARP HENU. All S.A.A. was transferred from DAE to IV corps ACHEUX previous move to new area. Reinforcements received during the month were 8 pack type. Remounts from DIEPPE were very good though in soft condition. 8 May 10th October 12th. Return during the month have been heavy. Forage ration was increased on 21.3.17. 8 May 10th October 12th. Return during the month have been heavy. Heavy work has been done on repairs of G.S. Wagons. This was rendered necessary by heavy work & bad condition of the roads. Health during the month good. Discipline of the month of the troops excellent.	

J.H. Hinton Lt. Col R.F.A.
O.C. 46 D.A.C.

WAR DIARY or INTELLIGENCE SUMMARY

Army Form C. 2118.

Place	Date	Hour	Summary of Events and Information	Remarks and references to Appendices
AENUS	5.3.17		20 Reinforcements arrived from Base & distributed to Brigades RFA 1-41 DAC.	
	9.3.17		63 Reinforcements arrived from DIEPPE & distributed to Brigades RFA & 46 DAC. 20 GSW 99 mortar teams proceeded to COURCELLES	
	10.3.17		to work on Roads under V Corps. S.S. W 90 mortar teams received at COLIN CAMPS & delivering ammn to APP. HENU 90 rounds TMR & 20 rounds TMF delivered to FONQUEVILLERS. 1600 No 23 Grenades delivered to FONQUEVILLERS. 5540 Rounds SAA + 2458 Bx delivered to 4 new portions occupied by Batteries in G.S. Wagons	
	11.3.17		24 Reinforcements arrived from Base & posted to 46 DAC.	
	12.3.17		2396 rounds A.5404 A.X. 1376 B.x sent up to Batteries/positions by pack animals. Reserves were all occupied in boxes at Nil	
	13.3.17		5846 No 5 grenades sure, No 23 grenades delivered to Renault. This SOUASTRE. Capt Martin was in charge R. SAA dump - issues were grenades + 5000 rds from Places of Infantry carrying parties to each Battery. Heavies to BIEZ Cart-Bosh animals also delivered 16000 rds Grenades - 20000 rounds SAA - 2500 (cartridges) + No 23 grenades to BIEZ	
			WOOD. 3016 A + 666 Bx were also delivered by pack animals to Batteries in action from a forward dump formed at	
			SAILLY AU BOIS. 2 G.S. Wagons with R.E. Material moved to PIGEON WOOD	
	14.3.17		Forward dump for 6 & 8 Batteries formed at SOUASTRE FORK. 6864 rounds A. 908 A.X. 472 Bx delivered from forward dump to 6 & 8 Batteries in action. This ammunition was delivered mostly by daylight - Carriers were laid	
	16.3.17		4904. A. 632. A.X. 6928.X. delivered from forward dumps to Batteries	
	16.3.17		1107 B A. 574.A.X. 468.B.x.	
	17.3.17		48 D.A.C. took over ammunition dumps at COIGNEUX form 31 DAC. 20 further teams with 2 ft minebroad to AUTHIE	
			MILL to 4 Reserve Park. 20 G.S. Wagons with 6 horse teams under Lt Wik attached to C.E. III Corps at COLIN CAMPS.	
			20 boxes from water dump within 15 rds supplied to 468 Field Company R.E.	
			66 rounds A. 468 Bx collected from forward R.E. Motors delivered to Batteries.	
	18.3.17		100,000 SAA delivered to Train. x at GOMMECOURT	
	22.3.17		1 A F A PEPPER + 32 OR Transferred to 165 A C from TM Batteries on abolition of W46 & 746 T.M. Batteries	
	25.3.17		A. Officer to Hospital Sick	
	26.3.17		1 B.O.R. Evacd to Hospital Sick	
	27.3.17		48 Reinforcements from Base for DAC. 136 Horses + 80 mules with harness sent to Brigades & Batteries	
			The march to New Area. 118 animals. We & harness drivers arrive from Brigades in exchange	
			Rose horses were used to pair augst wagons	
	28.3.17		10 Officers + 733 OR from T M Batteries absorbed by 46 DAC	
	29.3.17		A Echelon - French Mortars march to LE MEILLARD - B Echelon to MEZEROLLES.	

SECRET

--:--

WAR DIARY.

--:--:--

46th: DIVISIONAL AMMUNITION COLUMN.

--;--:--

MARCH 1st: to MARCH 31st: 1917.

--:--:--

WAR DIARY

46th DIVISIONAL AMMUNITION COLUMN

INTELLIGENCE SUMMARY.

Army Form C. 2118.

Place	Date	Hour	Summary of Events and Information	Remarks and references to Appendices
HENU.	26.2.17		47 F.A. Waggons supply Ammunition to Battery positions.	
	28.2.17.		30 O.Rs proceed to 3rd Army T.M. School.	

During the month the following Number of rounds of Ammunition have been delivered to Battery Positions
viz. A.8786 - A.X.4,298 - B.X.15,836 - T.H.B.3370 - T.H.F.260 - A.X.26.106
B.X.7468 were returned during the month.

The weather has been cold but dry with very hard frost. The health of the men has been excellent.
5 horses were evacuated for inspection & mange. The unit has been clear of all skin diseases amongst
horses since 15th of the month. Forage ration remains at 9 lbs of Oats & 10 lbs of Hay. Notwithstanding
this short ration - hard work & cold weather the horses on the whole have retained their condition.
The remounts received were all of good stamp.

Much repair work on R.S. Waggons has been done. He state of the roads after the thaw & the first
amount of fatigue work done to them was/was necessitated two difficulties experienced in keeping spare parts for Waggons
He also states that the waggons under all their wheels of transport are in excellent

A Hutton Capt RFA.
8e 46 DAC

WAR DIARY
46th DIVISIONAL AMMUNITION COLUMN
INTELLIGENCE SUMMARY

Army Form C. 2118.

Place	Date	Hour	Summary of Events and Information	Remarks and references to Appendices
HENU	6.2.17		40 G.S. Waggons from 49 B.A.C. arrive at Refilling point & assist in supply of Ammunition	
	10.2.17		16 O.R.s return from 3rd Army Trench Mortar School.	
			Lt. Balme + 24 O.Rs proceed to 3rd Army Trench Mortar School for Training.	
			70 G.S. Waggons convey ammunition to Battery positions 46 Div Arty.	
	11.2.17		94 G.S. Waggons — ditto —	
	12.2.17		97 G.S. Waggons — ditto —	
	13.2.17		116 G.S. Waggons — ditto —	
	14.2.17		105 G.S. Waggons collect Ammunition from Battery positions return to Refilling Point.	
	15.2.17		Leave extended indefinitely by War Office to Capt & Hon. Maj. J.P. Wood pending transfer to A.V.C.	
			Lieut Phillips F.J. Passed by Medical board - unfit for Active Service - Await orders War Office.	
			96 G.S. Waggons collect Ammunition from Battery positions & return to Refilling Point.	
	16.2.17		121 G.S. Wagons — ditto —	
	17.2.17		59 G.S. Wagons — ditto —	
			2/Lt M. Parker posted to 282 Brigade R.F.A.	
	18.2.17		40 G.S. Wagons returned to 49 B.A.C.	
			Lt. Balme + 28 O.Rs return from 3rd Army T.M. School.	
	20.2.17			
	21.2.17		2/Lt Parker reported to 460 D.A.C. from 282 Bde R.F.A.	
	25.2.17		96 Remounts arrived from DIEPPE & issued to vanish A.B. Brigades.	

Secret

CONFIDENTIAL.

WAR DIARY

46. DIVISIONAL AMMUNITION COLUMN.

FEBRUARY 1st: to FEBRUARY 28th: 1917.

WAR DIARY
or
INTELLIGENCE SUMMARY.
(Erase heading not required.)

Army Form C. 2118.

Place	Date	Hour	Summary of Events and Information	Remarks and references to Appendices
HENU.			The weather experienced during the month has varied from much rain & mud in the earlier days to snow & very hard frost in the latter half. The health & the men under all the circumstances has been very good. The animals have improved owing to the statning drier conditions. Rations with the exception of temporary shortage of oats have been excellent. During the month 1387 rounds A 283 H.X. 294 B.X. were collected from B: Kries returned to Railhead. These rounds were returned defective from various causes.	

J.B. Minton /Lt Col RFA
8/e 46 S.A.

WAR DIARY or INTELLIGENCE SUMMARY

Army Form C. 2118.

Place	Date	Hour	Summary of Events and Information	Remarks and references to Appendices
H.E.M.D.	26.1.17		2/Lt E.H. JOBBERNS joins from Base & is posted to Sect. I. 12 O.Rs. reinforcements from Base.	
	27.1.17		Capt. O.B. GILES to hospital, sick. F.G.C.M. held at HQ 46 D.A.C. on No. 5736004 "B" Echelon 2/Lt F. NELSON PARKER joins from Base via Abbeville & West II. Conf. Rate of 36 days F.P. No 1 passed on H.S. & Noon by F.G.C.M. promulgated. Verdict of 36 days F.P. No 1 passed on H.S. & Noon by F.G.C.M. promulgated.	
	30.1.12 31.1.12		During the month the following Ammunition has been distributed to Brigades. 2941 Rounds A. 6006 6550. A.X. 6058 Bx — 100 T.M.B. 173 T.M.F. 313000 S.A.A. Much work done on horse standings. Two complete standings built by Sect. I. Roads built up & round all standings & Sect. II. Existing standings all improved & drained. Work done on No 3. A.R.P. New standings constructed for Class F. Large shed covered revetted in new more convenient position for handling & returning empties. Sandbag traverses built between different classes of ammunition & outside ammunition sheds. Flooring & trench grids laid down in ammunition sheds. A Dump for R.E. Material established at No 3 H.R.P. for supply of Material to F.A. Brigades. All standings taken over were found thoroughly disinfected for Mange. Every part not covered — washed with creosote solution & white wash & every precaution taken to stamp out remote cause for infection. 21 animals leaving Remounts were inoculated from H.B. Serious either for Mange or suspected cases. Clipping of horses was carried out as rapidly as supply of clipping heads permitted to their indiscriminate use through & clear head of the discharge. Signalling classes were held twice daily for 2 Officers & 12 O.R's. A course of training — duration 14 days — was started for all new forces with a view to good results.	

WAR DIARY
or
INTELLIGENCE SUMMARY.
(Erase heading not required.)

Army Form C. 2118.

Place	Date	Hour	Summary of Events and Information	Remarks and references to Appendices
HENU	1.1.17.		Orders received to proceed with reorganisation of "A" Echelon in accordance with 3rd Army Ro. G8/14.	
	2.1.17.		"A" Echelon reduced from 3 sections to 2 - Sect III forming 232 B.A.C. (Army Field Artillery Brigade). Sect III forming Sect III 46 D.A.C. S.A.A. portions & female waggons from Sects I & II 232 B.A.C. removed and distributed to Sections I + II 46 D.A.C. Capt H.T. Banford to Lieut A. Hay transferred to 232 B.A.C. - 2/Lt V. Dixon posted Sect II 46 D.A.C. A.F.B. Bentley to Sect I. "B" Echelon 46 D.A.C. reduced by 30 O.R., 42 L.D horses + 7 Waggons G.S. which are transferred to 232 B.A.C.	
	3.1.17.		Two reinforcements from Base.	
	4.1.17.		Capt W.T. Wood to England on leave.	
	8.1.17.		232 B.A.C. remains under the 46 D.A.C. for administration. 1 Chaff cutter received from Ordnance.	
	9.1.17.		2/Lt C. Balme from Base posted to Sect II. 2/Lt J.V. Dixon posted from D.A.C. to 230 Siege B.A. 2/Lt Col. J. Winton to England on leave.	
	10.1.17.		S.O. R. from D.A.C posted to Trench Mortar Batteries.	
	18.1.17.		Oat Ration reduced from 12 lbs to 9 lbs per animal.	
	20.1.17.		"B" Echelon inspected by G.O.C. 46th Division. The G.O.C. expressed great pleasure at the "very marked improvement shown all round" since his last inspection & desired all Officers + O.Rs. B "B" Echelon to be informed of the fact. This was duly carried out.	

CONFIDENTIAL.

WAR DIARY.

46th: DIVISIONAL AMMUNITION COLUMN.

JANUARY 1st: to JANUARY 31st: 1917.

****

WAR DIARY
or
INTELLIGENCE SUMMARY.

(Erase heading not required.)

Army Form C. 2118.

Place	Date	Hour	Summary of Events and Information	Remarks and references to Appendices
MILLY.	14.12.16.		Capt Bentley M.F.C. from Base posted to 46 D.A.C. Lecture by G.O.C.R.A. 46th Div to all Officers of 46 D.A.C. Subject Discipline.	
	17.12.16		2/Lt Johnson L.V. to England to report to War Office.	
	20.12.16		46 D.A.C. move into future & relieve 49 D.A.C. H.Q to P.A.S. "A" Echelon to HENU. B Echelon to GRINCOURT. States standing up thoroughly transferred & surface turned with plow & cross provided for all horses but condition of midrings bad.	
	22.12.16		H.Q Move to HENU.	
	25.12.16		Div Arty Order 739. 2/Lt (Temp Capt) Bentley M.F.C. reverts to rank of Temp Lieut on posting to 46 D.A.C.	
			13.12.16 with seniority from 30. 11. 16.	
	27/12/16		40 Remounts arrived & distributed to "A" + B Echelons	

M. Whidon Mah RFA
OC 46 D.A.C.

Army Form C. 2118.

WAR DIARY
or
INTELLIGENCE SUMMARY.
(Erase heading not required.)

Instructions regarding War Diaries and Intelligence Summaries are contained in F. S. Regs., Part II. and the Staff Manual respectively. Title pages will be prepared in manuscript.

Place	Date	Hour	Summary of Events and Information	Remarks and references to Appendices
SAVY.	1.12.16		20 Reinforcements joined from Base reported to Sections of D.A.C. 2/Lt Graham E.F. posted to 231 Bde RFA. 2/Lt Birch D.J. posted to 232 Bde RFA. B. Echelon marched to new billets at LES ANNELLES FARM from COULLEMONT.	Total Reinforcements received during the month. 668 horses A. 3262 " A.X. 2626 " B.X. 6 " 8 PF. 650 " T.M.B. 22,000 O.R. T.A.A.
	3.12.16		A. Echelon marched to new billets at MILLY. 30th D.A.C. marched in to SAVY & took over No 1. A.R.P.	Weather
MILLY	4.12.16		While in training area 46 D.A.C. programme consisted:- Riding & Driving drill- Gun drill- Signalling - Musketry drill. Physical drill. Musketry - a Rifle Range was erected men of the unit went through the Grouping Test. All officers were in the open in men of the unit went through the Grouping Test. All offrogs NCOs & men attending the lectures. But owing to much frost & much snow which prevented hard attending. 15 G.S. Wagons daily were turned out for fatigue for artillery Brigades & 49 Division. Capt Bamford H.A. rejoined this day with 12 teams & 15 Riders from having C/242 BdeBy R.F.A. 48th Divn. These were down with Ringworm. These teams left COULLE MONT 8.0. am 30.12.16 marched to GRINCOURT & arrived in 6 Vehicles. They then marched to OCCOCHES arriving 3.p.m. Next day 1.12.16 they marched to VILLERS BOCAGE. 2.12.16 marched to PIEARGBT & remained until 9 a.m. 4.12.16 when they marched to rejoin 46 D.A.C. at MILLY. The march was in every way satisfactory. GOCRA 48th Divn congratulated Capt Bamford on the turn out & march discipline of his section.	Healthy the maneuvres has been fair
	6.12.16		Inspection parade near LUCHEUX B 46 D.A.C. was inspected by GOC 46Divn. 46 D.A.C. presented by O.C. adjt 2 officers & 80 O.Rs per section. After the Inspection the Troops marched part(dismounted) The G.O.C. 46 Divn expressed himself as pleased with the turn out & march past of the D.A.C. 2/Lt (Temp Capt) A.H.P. Clarke reverts to Rank of Temp Lieut on Posting 46 D.A.C. 29.11.16 with Seniority from 2/8/16. Lt Payne H. joined B. Echelon took over command from Capt Allen Major L.Who is temporarily attached to H.Q. 46 D.A.C.	
	14.12.16		12 Reinforcements from Base reported to B. Echelon - Physique fair. Equipment good but no Haversacks - Training - Regt men were issued & horses riddled to G.S. Manage & their lead only had 6 weeks training.	

A5534 Wt W4973/M687 750,000 8/16 D.D.&L.Ltd. Forms/C.2118/13.

Secret

CONFIDENTIAL.

--:--:--

WAR   DIARY.

--:--:--

46th: Divisional Ammunition Column.

--:--:--:--:--

December 1st: to December 31st: 1915.

WAR DIARY
or
INTELLIGENCE SUMMARY.
(Erase heading not required.)

Army Form C. 2118.

46th Div. Ammn Col

Hour, Date, Place	Summary of Events and Information	Remarks and References to Appendices
COULLEMONT. 1.11.16.	S.A.A. Section 46th D.A.C. consisting of 4 Officers, 240 O.R's, 44 G.S. wagons, 15 S.A.A. Carts, carrying 1,840,000 Rnds S.A.A. 115 Btts Grenades move to OCCOCHES. with 46th Divn. Inn Artillery	There is nothing special to report for the month of November. Officers N.C.O's have attended evening lectures during the month with satisfactory results.
SAULTY. 9.11.16.	Section 3. 46th D.A.Col moves to new billets from SAULTY. to COULLEMONT.	The reinforcements that arrived men & officers are suitable, bulk had little knowledge of Armaments, harness fitting &c.
" 10.11.16.	Section of D.A.C. attached to C/150 Bty R.F.A. join 46th D.A.C. — consisting of 24 O.R's 4/45 limbers, 4 G.S. wagons, 24 R.D. Horses, 24 mules & posted to Section 2.	Supplies have been adequate. Discipline very good.
" 10.11.16.	45 Remounts arrive from Dieppe, & distributed to Units in 46th Division.	Health of men have been good considering the inclement weather been experiencing.
" 21.11.16.	25 Reinforcements arrive from Havre & posted to Roles.	
" 25.11.16.	S.A.A. Section 46th D.A.C. rejoin 46th D.A.C. take over billets at COULLEMONT.	M Morrison Lt Col R.F.A. D.A.C. Commg 46th D.A.C.

SECRET

~~CONFIDENTIAL~~

WAR DIARY

46TH. DIVISIONAL AMMUNITION COLUMN

WAR DIARY
or
INTELLIGENCE SUMMARY.
(Erase heading not required.)

Army Form C. 2118.

Instructions regarding War Diaries and Intelligence Summaries are contained in F. S. Regs., Part II. and the Staff Manual respectively. Title pages will be prepared in manuscript.

Hour, Date, Place	Summary of Events and Information	Remarks and References to Appendices
24.X.16. SAULTY.	24 O.R's, 48 Horses, 4 G.S. wagons, 4 G.S. limbers to D.A.C from Base, being the extra complement allotted to D.A.C from the Battery. (512 Bde. R.F.A) on joining the 46" D. Arty.	
30.X.16. "	Section 3. 46" D.A. Col. provide personnel, horses for R.A. Training School. Sunday.	

WAR DIARY
or
INTELLIGENCE SUMMARY.

(Erase heading not required.)

Army Form C. 2118.

Place	Hour, Date	Summary of Events and Information	Remarks and References to Appendices
SAULTY.	3.10.16	Lt. Col. Challmis D.S.O. admitted to Hospital.	Officers, Senior N.C.O's (during the month) have attended a series of Lectures given by O.C. D.A.C. on Battery tactics, care & filling of harness, with satisfactory results. The reinforcements that have arrived during the month are of a fair sample, that is ten from lungs of Remount Depots, + horsematerials. Discipline has been good. The condition of horses remain in good considering the inclement weather experienced. The earth of all the remounts has been excellent Supplies have been adequate.
GAUDIEMPRE	8.10.16	Section B. 46" D.A.C. move from GAUDIEMPRE to SAULTY.	
WARLINCOURT.	6:10:16	Section H. 46" D.A.C. ("B" Echelon) move from WARLINCOURT to SONGAMP.	
SAULTY.	13:10:16	7 Reinforcements received from Base Depot.	
"	15:10:16	Major L.H. Hinton B/230 Bde. R.F.A. takes over command of 46" D.A. Col.	
"	14:10:16	7 Reinforcements received from Base Depot.	
"	19.10.16	2/Lt. F.A. Pepper 46" D.A. Col. posted to V H°. T.M. Battery.	
SONGAMP.	21:10:19	Section H. 46" D.A. Col. ("B" Echelon) move from SONGAMP to COULLEMONT.	
SAULTY.	22.10.16	34 Remounts received from DIEPPE + distributed to Brigades.	

A.H.Wilson
Comdg 46" D.A. Col. Major R.F.A.

CONFIDENTIAL.

WAR DIARY.

46th: DIVISIONAL AMMUNITION COLUMN.

October 1st: to October 31st: 1916.

WAR DIARY
or
INTELLIGENCE SUMMARY.
(Erase heading not required.)

Army Form C. 2118.

Hour, Date, Place		Summary of Events and Information	Remarks and References to Appendices
SAULTY.	21.9.16.	28 O.R.'s proceed to 3rd Army School of Motors for training.	Officers & O.R.'s during the month have received training in Gunmanship, harness fitting & bathing. Faith with satisfactory results. The reinforcements that have arrived during the month are of a good calibre. The knowledge of Gunmanship, & harness fitting & discipline during the month has been very good. The condition of the horses & mules has greatly improved. The health of all ranks has been good. Supplies have been adequate.
SOMBRIN.	22.9.16.	Section 2. (46th D.A.Col.) move from SOMBRIN to GAUDIEMPRE dump, for the purpose of collecting ammunition from un-manned gun positions.	
SOMBRIN.	24.9.16.	Section 4 ("B" Echelon) 46th D.A.Col. move from SOMBRIN to WARLINCOURT for the purpose of collecting ammunition from un-manned gun & returns.	
SAULTY.	25.9.16.	2/Lt. R.L. Johnson to 9.A.Col. from Base. 12 Reinforcements join from Base & posted to B.A.Col.	
"	26.9.16.	21 Remounts arrive from Drafts, redistributed to Brigade.	W.Watkin Lt.Col. R.F.A. Comdg. 46th D.A.C.

Army Form C. 2118.

WAR DIARY
or
INTELLIGENCE SUMMARY.
(Erase heading not required.)

Instructions regarding War Diaries and Intelligence Summaries are contained in F. S. Regs., Part II. and the Staff Manual respectively. Title pages will be prepared in manuscript.

Hour, Date, Place	Summary of Events and Information	Remarks and References to Appendices
SAULTY. 4.9.16	G.O.C. 4th Divn. inspects 4th D.A.Col. in field. Service Marching order.	
" 12.9.16	20. O.R's. transferred to D.A.Col. from Brigades (Surplus personnel).	
" 14.9.16	4. fitters transferred to D.A.Col. from Brigades in accordance with Brig. Army letter authorising an increase of 4 to D.A.C's organised on 6 gun basis.	
" 15.9.16	35 O.R's. from D.A.Col. attain 3 S.O.R's. with 4 sent Mnter Batteries.	
MONDICOURT 16.9.16	Section 2. (of 4th D.A.Col.) move from MONDICOURT to SOMBRIN, + provide personnel thereat for Artillery Training School.	
COULLEMONT 16.9.16	Section 4 ("B" Echelon) 4th D.A.Col. move from COULLEMONT to SOMBRIN.	

CONFIDENTIAL.

WAR DIARY.

46th: Divisional Ammunition Column.

SEPTEMBER 1st: to SEPTEMBER 30th: 1916.

Vol 20

WAR DIARY
or
INTELLIGENCE SUMMARY.
(Erase heading not required.)

Army Form C. 2118.

Hour, Date, Place	Summary of Events and Information	Remarks and References to Appendices
28/8/16. LAVITY.	4 Reinforcements to B.A.C. 1 Officer 36 O.R's to 2nd Army Schools T.M. Regs for instruction in the new Stokes T.M. Regs. 12. O.R's from B.A.C. transfers to 4 & 6th Div. and Meilan Batty's in accordance with 2nd Echelon letter. 1055/16. of 9th August.	
30/8/16. LAVITY.	Esten. B. 46th B.A.C. consisting of 3 Officers, 149 O.R's + 208 Animals proceeded to LE GROS TISON FARM to relieve section 1. 46th B.A.C. Personnel + horses required for the R.A. training School.	2/Lt Stallion Lt Cox R.F.A. +to D.A.C.

Army Form C. 2118.

WAR DIARY
or
INTELLIGENCE SUMMARY.
(Erase heading not required.)

Instructions regarding War Diaries and Intelligence Summaries are contained in F. S. Regs., Part II. and the Staff Manual respectively. Title pages will be prepared in manuscript.

Hour, Date, Place	Summary of Events and Information	Remarks and References to Appendices
19/8/16 S. AULTY.	The following Officers of the B.A.C. transferred to Brigades. 2/Lt R.H. Lund — 230" Brigade R.F.A. " O.G. Goatman — 231st Brigade R.F.A. " R.C. Northwaite " H. Winwood — 232nd Brigade R.F.A.	A large number of Officers have arrived from the B.A.C. during the month. Special instruction in horsemanship, Gunnery & Horse + Battery tactics have been given, with satisfactory results.
21/8/19 AULTY.	21. Reinforcements from Base. 20. D.A. Col.	
22/8/19 —	8 Remounts from DIEPPE to D.A. Col.	The Reinforcements that have arrived during the month have a good knowledge of horsemanship + horses actually.
24/8/19 —	4 Officers from Base, posted temporarily to B.A.C. 2/Lt. E. Chapman, 2/Lt G.H. Derwin, 2/Lt H.R. Heathcote 2/Lt D.S. Buck	
24/8/19 —	46 Remounts from Dieppe to B.A.C. + distributed to Bdes.	The condition of the horses similar to good.
9/8/52 —	2/Lt Heathcote } transferred to 30" Divl. Arty. " Hodge } on the reorganisation of the Divl. Arty.	The health of the men during the month have been good. Supplies have been adequate.

[Signature] Col. R.A.

WAR DIARY
or
INTELLIGENCE SUMMARY
(Erase heading not required.)

Army Form C. 2118.

Hour, Date, Place	Summary of Events and Information	Remarks and References to Appendices
SAULTY. 4/8/16	40 O.R's from Section of B.A.C. to Base, for the purpose of Lewis wire.	
7/8/16	Instructions received from the Gotel. G.H.Q. increasing "A" Echelon by 15, in order to meet the additional advance on the personnel of the B.A.Col, engaged in the inclusion of the Medium the adj. T.M. Btys, as an integral part of the Divis. Arty.	
8/8/16	21 O.R's proceed to 2nd Army School for instruction in Medium Heavy T.M. Battys.	
15/8/16	2 Officers from Base & Gotald. temporarily to B.A.Col viz:- 2/Lt. H. Wake, 2/Lt. F.R. Hodge.	
15/8/16	25 Reinforcements from Base.	

CONFIDENTIAL

WAR DIARY.

46th: DIVISIONAL AMMUNITION COLUMN.

AUGUST 1st: to AUGUST 31st: 1916.

Army Form C. 2118.

WAR DIARY
or
INTELLIGENCE SUMMARY.
(Erase heading not required.)

Instructions regarding War Diaries and Intelligence Summaries are contained in F.S. Regs., Part II. and the Staff Manual respectively. Title pages will be prepared in manuscript.

Hour, Date, Place		Summary of Events and Information	Remarks and references to Appendices
GRINGOURT.	3/4/10.	85 remounts to O.R. Coy. & distributed to Bns.	There is nothing of any importance to report. Often men have been a considerable time in camp without leaves. Future Lottery Tactical Scheme being arranged. Several Junior Officers have been attached to Batteries for instruction purposes. The condition of the horses in the main has greatly improved. The health of the men has been good. Leather during the month has been adequate. W. J. Mathison Comdr. H.Q. Coy.
GAUDIEMPRE.	4/4/10.	Analgm staff move from GAUDIEMPRE to SAULTY. Section 1 & 3 move from GRINGOURT to SAULTY.	
GRINGOURT.	"	O.A.G. takes over Ammun dump at SAULTY from 3rd Division.	
	5/4/10.	Section 4 ("B" Echelon) move from GRINGOURT to BOULLEMONT.	
GAUDIEMPRE.	14/4/10.	Staff moved south. GAUDIEMPRE and to 34th Divn.	
	15/4/10.	19 O.R. take over GAUDIEMPRE camp from 34th Divn.	
SAULTY.	24/4/10.	Gen. Parks. Sect. 3. "b" B.A.C. amalgamated 24/4/10. A.A. (2 years Impt. H.L.) 9(1)	
	31/4/10.	Section 1 40 O.R.s move to Le Gros Tison FARM for duties in the outpost to Stavenue per Lieut. H.Q. for R.A. Stavenue Sale O.C.	

CONFIDENTIAL.

WAR DIARY.

46th: DIVISIONAL AMMUNITION COLUMN.

July 1st: to July 31st: 1916.

Army Form C. 2118.

WAR DIARY
or
INTELLIGENCE SUMMARY.
(Erase heading not required.)

Instructions regarding War Diaries and Intelligence Summaries are contained in F.S. Regs., Part II and the Staff Manual respectively. Title pages will be prepared in manuscript.

Hour, Date, Place		Summary of Events and Information	Remarks and references to Appendices
GAUDIEMPRE.	26/6/16	L.D. Reinforcement received from N.M. Res. Dpt. 730 to B.A.C. 10 to Bde.	
	29/6/16	2. O.R.'s slightly wounded, 2 mules killed, + 2 wounded, whilst delivering ammunition.	27 Hollins Lieut Col. R.A. Commdg. 40th D.A.C.

WAR DIARY
or
INTELLIGENCE SUMMARY.
(Erase heading not required.)

Army Form C. 2118.

Hour, Date, Place		Summary of Events and Information	Remarks and references to Appendices
GRINCOURT.	1/6/16	H.Q. R.A. 1st Cdn. inspects 40th D.A. Col.	During the month this Unit have been delivering to Batty. positions also performing a various fatigues for G.R.E. 40th Div. An average of 80 teams daily (Sat. & 20th not) have been supplied.
"	4/6/16	Lieut. Col. Phallens. O.C. 40th D.A.C. awarded D.S.O.	
"	11/6/16	No. 818 Gnr. Dalby W. sent under escort to Military Prison Rouen to complete sentence of 2 years Impt. (Sect. 6 (11) A.A.).	Ammunition has been supplied direct from Ammunition dump.
"	22/6/16	90 Firements collected by D.A.C. to distribute to 40th Divsn.	
"	24/6/16.	Return of Hdqr. Staff Section 2. 40th D.A.C. moved to dump GAUDIEMPRE in ordnance unit in receiving ammunition from Hdqr. R.A. 40th Divn.	Batty. Gun positions entirely very few casualties have occurred.
HUMBERCOURT.		"B" Echelon 40th D.A.C. move from HUMBERCOURT to GRINCOURT	The health of the men has been good. The condition of the horses is kept up to full standard, owing to the heavy fatigues carried out. Supplies during the month have been adequate. Discipline has been good.
GAUDIEMPRE	25/6/16	2.O.R.'s of Sect. 2. 40th D.A.C. slightly wounded whilst delivering ammunition 3 mules killed, 3 wounded.	

CONFIDENTIAL.

WAR DIARY.

HEAD QUARTERS

46th: DIVISIONAL AMMUNITION COLUMN

JUNE 1st: to JUNE 30th: 1916.

Army Form C. 2118.

WAR DIARY
or
INTELLIGENCE SUMMARY.
(Erase heading not required.)

Instructions regarding War Diaries and Intelligence Summaries are contained in F. S. Regs., Part II and the Staff Manual respectively. Title pages will be prepared in manuscript.

Hour, Date, Place	Summary of Events and Information	Remarks and references to Appendices
HUMBERCOURT to GRINCOURT. 22/5/16.	Capt R.F. Martin, O.C. Sect. 2. (no change) O.R. Giles O.C. 1st Res. Am. Col. to Sect. 1. (4th D.A.C.) as O.C.	
GRINCOURT. 23/5/16.	D.A.C. collected all reinforcements for 40th Divl Arty. 48. Posted to D.A.C. remainder distributed to 230th, 231st, 232nd, 233rd Bdes. 44 Remounts to D.A.C. from 56? D.A.	
25/5/16.	44 Remounts from 394 D.A. to D.A.C.	
29/5/16.	9 Remounts from 134th Bde. R.F.A. to D.A.C.	
31/5/16.	Promulgation of G.C.M. on Gun. Dalby. W. sentence 5 years P.S. entrenchments remitted to 2 years Impt. H.L.	

W.T. Baldwin Lt Col. RHA
Comdg. 40?

(73989) W4141—463. 400,000. 9/14. H.&J.Ltd. Forms/C. 2118/10.

WAR DIARY
or
INTELLIGENCE SUMMARY.

(Erase heading not required.)

Army Form C. 2118.

Hour, Date, Place	Summary of Events and Information	Remarks and references to Appendices
HUMBERCOURT. 18/5/16.	Lt.Col. H. Y. Challiner, R.M.A. H. M. Roe. R.F.A. to D.A. Col. as O.C. D.A.C.	
" 22/5/16. to GRINCOURT.	Reorganization of the old D.A.C. & attached R. & F.A. Am. Columns on a Sectional basis in accordance with army letter No SS.40/11/Ma. "A" Echelon 46th D.A.C. (consisting of Hdqrs. Sections 1, 2, & 3. Proceed to new Billets at GRINCOURT. "B" Echelon consisting of Sect in remain at HUMBERCOURT. following officers join HdQrs D.A.C. on reorganization. Capt. O.R. Guise Smart. (Late Am. Col.) 2/Lieut. E.L. Lund. Am. Res. Cte. " A.R. Lund. 2nd " " S.H. Nunn " " E.W. Smart broken to Sect. 1 " B.A. Lund " 2 " J.H. Nunn " 3 The following strength of Section Commdrs. one the Reorgany obtn. Capt. WT Banford formerly O.C. Sect. 1 Capt. (Hon. Maj.) S.H. Nord formerly O.C. Sect 2 as O.C. Sect 1, as O.C. Sect 2 for section 3 an O.C.	

WAR DIARY
or
INTELLIGENCE SUMMARY

(Erase heading not required.)

Army Form C. 2118.

Instructions regarding War Diaries and Intelligence Summaries are contained in F.S. Regs., Part II and the Staff Manual respectively. Title pages will be prepared in manuscript.

Hour, Date, Place	Summary of Events and Information	Remarks and references to Appendices
MAISNIL ST. POL. 1/5/16	2 Lieuts. E. Winwood & H.R. D.A. Col. transferred to 3rd H.M. Bde. R.F.A. Lieut F.S. Gunston from 3rd H.M. Bde. to 46th D.A.C. Lieut F. Phillips & 46 D.R.'s return from PRENIN-CAPELLE after completing the future of was buried for the 1st Highland Bde R.F.A.	As will be seen from the Diary the 2nd Am. Col. (46th Divn.) has been reconstructed into Divnonal Ammun Col. A & B Echelon, composed of 2 Echelon, of the strength of each Section 1, 2, & 3. ("B" Echelon Section 1, 2, & 3.) The necessary transfers & movements completed May 22nd 1916. From May 22nd 1916 Regn. the organization this is nothing special to report. Reinforcements have been received to complete the Estab., the men during the month have been subjected to adjusters. Drills etc. has been good. The health of men has been good.
" 4/5/16	S.A.A. Portion of Section 1 46 D.A.C. consisting of 10 Officers, 1 4 D.R's & wagons R.S. 4S Horses, proceeded to GUOY-EN-TERNOIS, in attachment to 13th Infantry Bde. Summary of evidence from a J.G.C.M. taken on Driver Taylor Rowden Section 2, 46th D.A.C. (Sect 9(2) A.A).	
" 7/5/16	Summary of evidence on a J.G.C.M. Gunner Daily W. Sect. 1, 46th S.A.C. (Sect 6 (1f) A.A.)	
" 8/5/16	D.A. Col. march to new Billets at HUMBERCOURT	
HUMBERCOURT 10/5/16	Promulgation of J.G.C.M. on Driver Taylor Rowden sentence of 3 months F.P. No. 1.	
	1 Officer & 40 O.R.'s (Working Party) proceed to GOUY & TRE.	
" 15/5/16	Maj. F.S. Whiteley (Outgrg 46th D.A.C.) transferred to 64th Batty 2nd H.M. Bde. R.F.A.	
	S.A.A. Section of Sect. 1 46 D.A.C. return.	

CONFIDENTIAL

WAR DIARY.

DIVISIONAL AMMUNITION COLUMN.

May 1st: to 31st: 1916.

Army Form C. 2118.

WAR DIARY
or
INTELLIGENCE SUMMARY.
(Erase heading not required.)

Instructions regarding War Diaries and Intelligence Summaries are contained in F. S. Regs., Part II. and the Staff Manual respectively. Title pages will be prepared in manuscript.

Hour, Date, Place	Summary of Events and Information	Remarks and references to Appendices
VILLERS BRULIN. 22/4/16	D.A.C. move to hew billets at MAISNEL ST POL.	
MAISNEL ST POL. 23/4/16	10 gun. 4.5.O.R. horses to run to. Highland Div. R.F.A. FREVIN-CAPELLE for burial of horses. Burying mice.	
24/4/16	10 gun. Q.D.R. ngn Column from Ammunition Dump. ACG 10 gun. 4.5.O.R. 8 wagons & S. 48 three mules return from CAPELLE-FREMONT on completion on fatigue.	
30/4/16	Section 2. 4.6" D.A. Col. ngn Column from Divisional fatigue at ECOIVRES	

Command... [signature]

WAR DIARY
or
INTELLIGENCE SUMMARY.
(Erase heading not required.)

Army Form C. 2118.

Instructions regarding War Diaries and Intelligence Summaries are contained in F.S. Regs., Part II and the Staff Manual respectively. Title pages will be prepared in manuscript.

Place	Hour, Date	Summary of Events and Information	Remarks and references to Appendices
Wen. Poulin	1/1/16	Park of station. 4 of No. D.A. Col. consisting of 1 Officer, 250 O.R. 30 mules 2 timing carts. Proceeded to ECOIVRES in the outskirts of hauling hinders of the 60 c/m railway.	There is nothing of interest to report. As seen from the Diary a large percentage of the Column have been on detached work.
"	2/1/16	2/Lt. A.E. Gostman + 2/Lt. B.S. Graham rejoin 146 D.A. Am. Col. from N.M. Base Depot.	The strength of Section 1, 2 + 3 Helgr. have been increased on the absorption of Section 4. Vide War Estab. NEW ARMIES Part VII. 1915
"	3/1/16	2/Lt. R.E. Barthwaite + 2/Lt. J.H. Timmons rejoin 146 D.A. Am. Col. from N.M. Base Depot. 14 O.R. from 146 B.M. Base Depot join after attachment to 1st — 2nd — 3rd — 4th.	Supplies during the month have been adequate.
			Other construction of dug-outs
	4/1/16	1 Officer + 9 O.R. proceed to A.C.Q. to form advanced ammun. dump. 1 Officer + 22 O.R. proceed to LIGNY ST FLOCHEL Station on Latrines.	The health of men + horses has been good. Discipline has been good.
	10/1/16	Section 4 (strs.) of 146 D.A. Col. absorbed into Other Sections. Reformation new Estab. (New Armies Part VII) 1915 in the following proportions:	

	Sec. 1	Sec. 2	Sec. 3	
Offers.	1	1	1	
17 O.R.	15 O.R.	17 O.R.	
2 Pairs	2 Pairs	2 Pairs	
22 mules	22 "	22 "	
3 wagons G.S.	3 "	3 "	
H.dqrs — 2 O.R.			

Mayn Rfa
146th D.A.C.
Commdg.

CONFIDENTIAL

WAR DIARY.

46th: DIVISIONAL AMMUNITION COLUMN

APRIL 1st: to 30th: 1916.

Army Form C. 2118.

WAR DIARY
or
INTELLIGENCE SUMMARY.
(Erase heading not required.)

Instructions regarding War Diaries and Intelligence Summaries are contained in F.S. Regs., Part II and the Staff Manual respectively. Title pages will be prepared in manuscript.

Hour, Date, Place	Summary of Events and Information	Remarks and references to Appendices
16/3/16. MONCHY. BRETON.	10 ???, 43 O.R. 10 wagons G.S. 60 horses marched to CAPELLE-FREMONT on Divnl. fatigues.	
17/3/16	14. O.R. to 1st N.M. Bde ⎫ 9. " " 2nd " " ⎬ for the construction 11. " " 3rd " " ⎪ of dug-outs. 9. " " 4th " " ⎭	
	Lt. R.C. Lewis posted to (SAC) transferred to 2nd H.M. Bde. R.F.A. Lt. J.L. Phillips from 2nd H.M. Bde. R.F.A. to 40th D. Col.	
28.3.16	2 Officers, 98 O.R. 152 horses, 21 wagons G.S. proceed to ECOIVRES on Divnl. fatigues.	
29.3.16	D.A.C. move from MONCHY. BRETON. to VILLERS-BRULIN.	

Army Form C. 2118.

46th D.A.C

WAR DIARY
or
INTELLIGENCE SUMMARY.
(Erase heading not required.)

Instructions regarding War Diaries and Intelligence Summaries are contained in F.S. Regs., Part II. and the Staff Manual respectively. Title pages will be prepared in manuscript.

Hour, Date, Place	Summary of Events and Information	Remarks and references to Appendices
2.3.16. FIGNVILLERS.	Section 2, 46th D.A. Col. rejoins D.A.C. from attachment to 53rd Divn.	There has been several changes in Billets during the month & that will systematic Route marches has given both Officers & men a good knowledge of march discipline, from which they have greatly benefited. Supplies during the month have been adequate. The health of men & horses has been good. Discipline has been good. M Murray Lt Col R.A. cmdg 46th DAC
6.3.16 —— ——	40th D.A. Col. move from FIGNVILLERS to MONTS-EN-TERNOIS.	
7.3.16 MONTS-EN-TERNOIS	2/Lieut R. Whittles 40th D.A. Col. transferred to Headquarters 11th Corps Park.	
8.3.16 —— ——	Section IV. 40th D.A.C. rejoins DAC from attachment to 55th Divisn.	
9.3.16 —— ——	1 Officer, 8 O.R. to French Motor School for motor tractors purposes.	
11.3.16 —— ——	D.A.C. move from MONTS-EN-TERNOIS to MONCHY-BRETON. No. 31500, R.S.M. Henry promoted Hon Lieut. to England. 11-3-16. No. 336. B.S.M. Nicholson T. appointed a/ R.S.M. vice Henry.	
15.3.16 MONCHY-BRETON.	10 Remounts to 46th D.A. Col.	

CONFIDENTIAL

WAR DIARY.

46th: DIVISIONAL AMMUNITION COLUMN

March 1st: to 31st: 1916.

Instructions regarding War Diaries and Intelligence Summaries are contained in F. S. Regs., Part II. and the Staff Manual respectively. Title pages will be prepared in manuscript.

WAR DIARY
or
~~INTELLIGENCE~~ SUMMARY.
(Erase heading not required.)

Army Form C. 2118.

Kmc

Hour, Date, Place	Summary of Events and Information	Remarks and references to Appendices
5th Feb 1916 L'ETOILE	17 OR attached to Trench Mortar School for instruction	[illegible]
12th Feb 1916 L'ETOILE	18 pr portion of Sec III + [illegible] Sections consisting of 2 offrs 101 OR 20 Wagons [illegible] 146 animals [illegible] DAC Temporary	
13th Feb 1916 L'ETOILE	63 Reinforcements from Base [illegible] distributed to [illegible]	
16th Feb 1916 L'ETOILE	[illegible] (How [illegible]) [illegible] [illegible] from Base	
18th Feb 1916 L'ETOILE	D A C [illegible] LARCHE [illegible] ST [illegible] BAC Portion [illegible] attached to [illegible] Temporary	
20th Feb 1916 [illegible]	57 Remounts from Base to D A C for distribution to Div	
21st Feb 1916 [illegible]	68 Reinforcements to D A C from Base distributed to [illegible]	
25th Feb 1916 [illegible]	[illegible] OR [illegible] [illegible] D A C from [illegible] [illegible] by [illegible] for [illegible]	
29th Feb [illegible]	D A C [illegible] 21 OR Reinforcements [illegible] D A C	

3 [illegible] complete

[signature]

CONFIDENTIAL

WAR DIARY.

DIVISIONAL AMMUNITION COLUMN.

FEBRUARY 1st: - 29th: 1916.

Vol XIII

Such shifting about leads to loss of kit
& parts of harness, especially when the
unit or part of unit arrives at the
Camp in the dark.

About 20% of the men were vaccinated
before leaving Luton, — no objection being
made by any. This was probably
due to the impression that successful
vaccination carried with it a week's
leave.

12.3.15.

B W Leach Lt Col.
OC 2/M Bac.

The training during the month was continued on the same lines, but the progress made was not commensurate with the time, due to a lack of energy among the N.C.O's & men. They did not or would not realise that the column was likely to go abroad in a short time, & saw no reason to stir themselves. — The continual changing of horses owing to sickness was also detrimental, the men having to be continually changed on to fresh horses. — The column continued up to the last doing transport work for the Reserve Units.

The entrainment for Southampton was very satisfactorily carried out. Help to load the wagons was given by the Reserve Artillery units. So that with end loading trucks there was no delay, & every train was ready to start at least half an hour before the scheduled time of departure.

It would have been more convenient if the whole column could have been embarked on the same ship, & put on board straight from the train instead of being sent to the Rest Camp for one night

Feb. 28 (cntd) to replace those cast were supplied by Remounts, Swaythling. Rations & forage drawn for four days. Stable picquets, guards over gangway & stores, and sanitary detachment told off. No officer or men allowed off the ship after 7.0 p.m. Lights at 9.15

Crieve Coeur Farm,
7/3/15.

T. W. Bellamy,
2° Lieut. & Actg. Adjt.
N. Mid. Div. Amm. Col.

Feb. 25	53 Mark X wagons arrived. The ammunition was transferred to them from the old wagons. Books of instruction for entrainment and embarkation received.
Feb. 26	Received time-table of special trains for move. Trainloads told off, 8 in number. 10 new Mark X wagons arrived in morning, and were taken over. Remainder arrived late in evening, and were left, owing to impossibility of transferring ammunition in time.
Feb. 27	Special trains all got off punctually, and reached Southampton docks at 2-hr. intervals from 2 a.m. to 4 p.m. The wagons were put on board ship, men and horses going to the Rest Camp. The first 7 trainloads were told off to S.S. Archimedes, the last — Headquarters and Sect. IV Heavies — to S.S. Caledonia.
Feb. 28	Men and horses embarked at 9.30 a.m on Archimedes (Capt. Nicol in command) and at 10.30 on Caledonia (Col. Leach commanding); details as above. Horses to complete deficiencies and

56

Feb. 22nd (cont.)	of the ground the wagons were parked on the road adjoining the stables. Orders received for Ammunition Park Section to begin at 9.58 a.m. on 23rd inst. for AVONMOUTH. Special orders issued about Rations, Desertion, and the fitting of poles of wagons.
Feb. 23rd	The Ammunition Park Section left by special train for AVONMOUTH. The train was delayed in starting as the Railway Company was only warned to provide trucks for 50 tons ammunition, whereas about 120 tons arrived and had to be sent off. Special orders issued as to attached A.S.C. men, and the Guard, each Section in future to find its own sentry and relief.
Feb. 24th	No parades ordered, the Sections being left to their Officers in preparation for move. Instructions received that the Column would be conveyed on Saturday, Feb. 27, in eight trains to port of embarkation. Special orders issued as to Rations, Forage, payment of billets, and distribution of ammunition in wagons.

Feb. 18th (cont'd)	from that unit arrived to make up deficiencies
Feb. 19th	Nature of training as above.
The remaining 15 pr. B.L.C. ammunition, required to complete issue, arrived.
92 Heavy draught and 9 riding horses arrived from Remounts, Market Harboro'.
Feb. 20th	Nature of training as above.
Men's kit-bags, surplus kit, and second blankets handed in.
The Column paraded in marching order for inspection by the Officer Commanding.
The harness to complete Section IV was issued, and fitted to the horses.
8 riding horses arrived in the evening.
Feb. 21st	Sunday — no training.
The new horses were issued to the Sections.
Special orders issued about absence without leave, and about Active Service Pay Books.
9 A.S.C. wagons for baggage arrived by special train
Feb. 22nd	Nature of training as above.
The Column paraded in marching order as for moving off. On account of the softness

Feb.12" (cont'd)	vaccinated. 10% of men went on leave.
Feb.13"	Saturday – half-holiday. Training as above.
Feb.14"	Sunday – no training.
Feb.15"	Nature of training as above. Major Mottram returned to 2/1st N.M.R.G.A. 2nd Lieut. H.W. Ballamy appointed acting adjutant.
Feb.16"	Nature of training as above. Brigade Route March. Route – via Stopsley towards Hitchin – through Butterfield Green to Luton – about 20 miles. The G.O.C.R.A inspected the Column on the march.
Feb.17"	Nature of training as above. Clothing and necessaries issued to complete men's equipment for moving.
Feb.18"	Nature of training as above. All sick horses were sent to the Veterinary Hospital, in readiness for the move. 35 men medically unfit for war service were transferred to the 2/2nd N.M. Bde R.F.A.: 28 men

Feb. 6th (cont'd)	horses 3 times per day at early stables, on return from morning parade, and at afternoon stables.
Feb. 7th	Sunday - no training.
Feb. 8th	Nature of training as above. Brigade Route March. Distance about 10 miles. Delivered 12 guns to Markyate for the 2/2nd N.M. Bde. R.F.A. 49 Heavy draught horses arrived.
Feb. 9th	Nature of training as above. 66 heavy draught horses arrived. New horses distributed amongst the sections.
Feb. 10th	Nature of training as above. Harness fitted to new horses.
Feb. 11th	Nature of training as above. Brigade Route March. Route - New Bedford Rd Round Green - Stopsley - Luton. Distance about 10 miles.
Feb. 12th	Nature of training as above. 20% of men

North Midland Divisional Ammunition Column

Date	Summary of Events & Information	Remarks
1915 Feb. 1st	Nature of training as follows — Early morning stables. Riding, driving and exercising horses in morning. Stables and harness cleaning in afternoon.	
Feb. 2nd	Training as above. Brigade Route March — distance covered about 10 miles. Route — New Bedford Rd and Leagrave.	
Feb. 3rd	Nature of training as above. Major Orme returned to 2/3rd N.M.Bde R.F.A.	
Feb. 4th	Nature of training as above. Brigade Route March. Distance & Route as on 2nd inst. Special orders issued as to Shoulder Titles, Exercising Sick Horses, & Night Alarm.	
Feb. 5th	Nature of training as above.	
Feb. 6th	Saturday. Half-holiday. Nature of training as above. Special orders as to watering	

121/4611

North Midland Division

NM Divisional Amm'n Col'n

Vol I. 1 – 28.2.15

Page 59 – No objection made to vaccination
if resulting in a week's leave –

Army Form C. 2118.

WAR DIARY
or
INTELLIGENCE SUMMARY.
(Erase heading not required.)

Instructions regarding War Diaries and Intelligence Summaries are contained in F.S. Regs., Part II. and the Staff Manual respectively. Title pages will be prepared in manuscript.

Hour, Date, Place	Summary of Events and Information	Remarks and references to Appendices
January 16th 1916 WITNESSED PONT REMY	Horse and equipment taken over from LAHORE D.A.C. by C in J Matthew. Horses, wagons, equipment of 46 D.A.C. handed on to LAHORE D.A.C. 46 D.A.C. now to be at SS & Division.	On the completion of the exchange the 46 Div. ammn Column consisted of 91 wagons and 688 horses and mules.
January 17th 1916 PONT REMY	Following men arrived as 46 D.A.C. representing a D.A.C. on the Reserve of officers. Lieut. Aitken L.R.A.D at LIERCOURT and ERONDELLE. Report from WITTERNESS.	Representing a D.A.C. on the Reserve Army basis) The normally 46 horses are brought from WITTERNESS & are supplied immediately by studying horses, relieved by studying horses to Artillery Bdes. & wagons to Artillery Bdes. and withdrawn
January 20th 1916 L'ETOILE	The Column arrived at L'ETOILE and marched to L'ETOILE on Jan 26th 1916. Designation changed from 55th Division (13 Lances) Div Ammn Col. to 46th Div Ammn Col.	Supports Bdes and withdrawn were received to march from LIERCOURT. The balance of the supplies and supplies to 46 at ERONDELLE and handed over to an officer from the 2nd W. Lancs 13th R.F.A Companies, the Clm left LIERCOURT on a route march being on approx 150 men. strictly are 85 men under strength.
January 30th 1916	Force of N.G./Sgt Witham being Commander (attached HQ 1st Corps. C.M. 307) N.M. Bdes R.F.A. returned to 46 D.A.C.	We have a plan of the Clm to has buried food, and supplies and rifles, a long at month.

Matthew
Major RFA
(in O.J.) 46th Div Ammn Col.

46th Div: Amm: Column

WAR DIARY
or
INTELLIGENCE SUMMARY.
(Erase heading not required.)

Army Form C. 2118.

Hour, Date, Place	Summary of Events and Information	Remarks and references to Appendices
January 1st 1916 WITTERNESS	2/Lt R Whittle rejoined DAC from 1st B" RFA. 4th H RFA. 2/Lt R Sudlow rejoined DAC from 3rd B" RFA. 4th H RFA. 2/Lt C H Cartwright Posted to 1st H" B" RFA. 2/Lt F H Padmore Posted to 3rd N H B" RFA. 2/Lt H F Smith Posted to 3rd N H B" RFA.	There has been a great many changes in officers + OR during the month. The taking & knowing over of horses wagons + equipment was done with difficulty & many with amm: columns not as intended down to the D.A.C. between him & the regular army without Brigades being at present was also
January 5th 1916 WITTERNESS	42 OR Posted to Base. 52 OR Posted to D.A.C. from Base.	
January 8th 1916 WITTERNESS	1/Lt fk Brumby attached to 4th B" A.C. to proceed overseas + in charge of amm: party from D.A.C. + NCO's 20 horses 31 OR Posted to Base to proceed overseas BSM Biggs th reduced under AA 1.53 (8)	
January 14th 1916 WITTERNESS	7 SSm on Sgt Wickham AA Sp 14	proceeded & training was all new horses was good. references for an officer + him
January 10th 1916 WITTERNESS	Orders received to exchange horses wagons + equipment with LAHORE D.A.C.	
January 15th 1916 WITTERNESS	5 Ofr + 150 OR proceeded by rail to Toot Remi to take over horses wagons + equipment LAHORE D.A.C. Promotion 1/S Cpl 1 yr Estimason Petterson to Cpl	

4611 Div Auen Col
Jan 96
Vol XII

WAR DIARY
or
INTELLIGENCE SUMMARY.
(Erase heading not required.)

Army Form C. 2118.

1/6th L is Amm Column

Hour, Date, Place	Summary of Events and Information	Remarks and references to Appendices
December 19th	Lt C R Chambers & 2/Lt H F Boucher joined from Base	1 - present billets between one on 2 x at all times. Horses are under cover, the hay has been improved by the change in number of each man received by Billeting discipline has improved. Supplies regular - Saluting
December 21st	Lt C R Chambers & 2/Lt H F B onchen posted to 2nd Bde	
December 22nd	Column marched to new billets at N 6 (WITTERNESS)	
December 23rd	Capt & T Ludlow posted to DAC from 3rd Bde to take command - Capt H J Banford taken over comd of sec I	
December 25th	2/Lt R Ludlow joined from Base	
December 27th	2/Lt S J Smith & 2/Lt E H Padman joined from Base	
December 28th	2/Lt R Ludlow posted to 3rd Bde	

[signature] Capt. R.F.A.
Comdg 1/6 L/BAC

Army Form C. 2118.

WAR DIARY
or
INTELLIGENCE SUMMARY.
(Erase heading not required.)

1/6th /s in Amln Column

Instructions regarding War Diaries and Intelligence Summaries are contained in F.S. Regs., Part II. and the Staff Manual respectively. Title pages will be prepared in manuscript.

Hour, Date, Place	Summary of Events and Information	Remarks and references to Appendices
December 1st 1915	18 G.S. wagons comptd Limbers taken over from Base this increase wagon per 1st to Amln from 24 to 42	After has been serious change in G.S. during the month owing to exchange 18pr for 15pr & 2.5" for 5" hows
December 4th	Lt Col RP Stack to ENGLAND on sick leave. Capt HT Bromyard taken over Command of Column	Hds have been exchanged for 1 D vehicles at first for the driving of 1 D now not gives owing to the introduction of a number of improvements.
December 5th	Column marched to hin billets at T.21	
December 6th	2/Lt J.B. Murdoch & 2/Lt R.S. Arrowsmith & 2/Lt A.V. Maddock joined from Base	Coin appreciably too have taken to get them on the road for instruction in driving. They are now good — a number of officers have joined known in the Bdes
December 7th	115 O.R. reinforcements joined from Base. H.D. exchanged for L.D. & all teams in GC wagon increased to 6 Horses	
December 9th	2/Lt R.S. Arrowsmith & 2/Lt A.V. Maddock posted to 2nd Bde RFA. Lt L. Uglow joined Column from 5th Corps H.Q.	
December 10th	Production of Ams in dismounted marching order by G.O.C. 46 W/Div.	
December 12th	See TC reduced to 6 wagons for hows Amln — See 1275. increased by 1 wagon each for S.A.A.	Stanhope Capt R.F.A. Andy O.C/Lt 1/6 [illegible] RFA
December 16th	5" Hows amln exchanged for 4.5"	

CONFIDENTIAL.

WAR DIARY.

46th
DIVISIONAL AMMUNITION COLUMN.

DECEMBER 1st: to 31st: 1915.

Vol XI

A 6 D'S Am. Col.
Dec. 1915

Statement.

The month has been uneventful, except for the various changes of billets.

Since arriving at the present billet the column has been almost exclusively employed on fatigues for other units. Although this has given regular work both to men & horses it has militated against work being done on horse standings, improvement of mens billets &c. On arrival at ST QUENTIN the column resumed the "Supply of ammn" to the Bde Cols which had temporarily been carried out by the Park direct.

The number of sick has increased during the month, due to the wet & cold weather. This is likely to continue until it is possible to make the mens barns weather tight, & get road ways &c constructed. Drying rooms for the men's clothes it is hoped will be in use shortly.

Discipline has been good, the horses are in good condition, & all supplies regular & satisfactory

1.12.15

R W Leach Lt Col
OC 46th DAC.

46th Div Amn Column
Summary of Events & Information

Nov 22nd — Remainder of 15pr Amn returned to Rlyhead & then made up with 18/2

Nov 23rd — 2/Lt Arthwright & 17 OR joined from Base

Nov 24th — F G C M on Cpl Hemple

Nov 24th — Inspection by Corps Commander

Nov 25th — Promulgation of F G C M Cpl Hemple reduced to Ranks & 3 mths F P No 1

Nov 30th — Orders received to take over from Bties 15 G S wagons complete transits

46th D.W. Amn Column
Summary of Events & Information

Nov 4th Column marched to new billets at LES-AMUSOIRES

Nov 10th 2/Lt Siblin & 1 OR joined from Base

Nov 13th 2/Lt Foster joined from Base

Nov 13th Column marched to new billets at ST FLORIS
          2/Lt Woodhouse to 1st Bde Posted
          2/Lt Siblin to 4th Bde Posted

Nov 16th 2/Lt Blyghton & 2/Lt Lawson joined from Base

Nov 17th 2/Lt L'Arcy-Evans to 2nd Bde
          "   Lawson to 1st Bde   ⎫
          "   Foster to 3rd Bde   ⎬ Attached
          "   Blyghton to 4th Bde ⎭
          Column marched to new billets at QUENTIN

Nov 17th One half of 15pr Ammn returned to R/head & 18/pr received in exchange

Hmc

Confidential.

War Diary
of
46. Divl. Amm: Col:

from 1st to 30th November
1915

46th Div. Ammn. Col.

Nomi.

Vol X

12/7694

46th Div Amn Column
Summary of Events & Information

Oct 14th A train of 2/Lt Woodhouse & 50 OR rejoined

Capt Bamford 50 OR sent up to trenches

Capt Martin wounded slightly accidental

Trench How party rejoined

Oct 15th Capt Bamford & 50 OR returned

Oct 18th Inspection of Clm in marching order by G.O.C. arty

Lieut TL rejoined from 7th Div. A.C.

Inspection of all Officers & OR who did duty in trenches

Oct 20th The sentence of 12 months H.L. (Suspended) on No 268 Gr Shore R remitted for gallant conduct on night of 13th/14th

Oct 28th 4 Officers & 33 OR inspected by the King

Oct 29th Reinforcements 45 OR from Base

Oct 30th 2/Lt St. G. W. D'arcy Evans from Base

46th F.A. Amtn Column
Summary of Events & Information

2nd Oct Clm marched out to VIEUX
BERQUIN night march

SAA portion of Sec II joined 2nd Bde AC

3rd Oct Clm marched to LE CORNET
BOUROIS night march

6th Oct SAA portion Sec II rejoined from
2nd Bde AC

4th Oct Clm marched out at 1030 AM
to take over Billets at LABEUVRIERE

8th Oct Reinforcements from Base 75 OR

12th Oct Capt R.F Martin & 11 OR attached
137th Inf Bde for trench How work,
Sec IV under Lt Lowndes attd
7th Div Amtn Column

13th Lt train 2/Lt Woodhouse 50 OR to trenches
carrying party
35 OR in addition sent up as stretcher
bearers

in good condition, & the health of the men very good in spite of the bad weather, & many of the men having to sleep in bivouacs All supplies have been regular & ample

1.11.15.

RW Leach Lieut
OC 46th DAC

Statement.

During the month the column was kept very busy, & gained useful experience. The two night marches were under very different conditions — the first on a bright moonlight night on good roads, the second on very bad roads in pitch darkness. —

For several days every available man was employed in preparing grenades for the Infantry, from 44 – 45 thousand being filled ready with detonators.

On 13th & 14th large parties of men with Officers were sent up to the trenches for carrying duties, gaining their first experience of coming under rifle fire. The behaviour of the men was excellent & one man especially distinguished himself (Gunner. E. Shone) one man was seriously wounded & one Officer (Capt R. F. Martin) slightly.

Discipline has been well maintained — the horses kept

121/7570

46th Division

4th Ammunition Col.

Oct 1915

Vol IX

with another Div" was satisfactorily carried out

Discipline has been good — The horses are in good condition, although there are still cases of mud ulcers

Supplies of all kinds have been adequate
There is a certain amount of waste in the issue of tobacco, as it is rare to see a man smoking a pipe. Cigarette smoking appears to be universal

Oct 4th 1915

R W Leach Lt Col
OC 46th DAC

Statement

The most important event of the month was the reduction in wagons, horses & men, reducing by one half the amount of Artillery Ammn carried by the column. Provided supply can be maintained by the Park, it is not anticipated that any difficulty will be experienced in keeping up the supply to the Bde Columns, although double work will be thrown on the men & horses, especially in the event of heavy fighting. The question of time is worthy of consideration. I calculate that assuming the Bde Columns to be distant 5 miles in front of the DAC, & the roads are fair, not more than 65 rounds 15pr every 5 hours could be supplied per gun. Is this sufficient? If not the number of wagons must be increased again. Recently small arm wagons have had to be used to meet calls for Howitzer ammn. Had there been heavy calls for SAA, difficulty would have been experienced.

The reduction of personnel & horses is serious as both are difficult to replace, & H D horses scarce.

Otherwise there is nothing special to record with regard to the Column. The change of area

WAR DIARY - 46th Divl Ammun Column

Summary of Events & Information
46th D.A. Ammn Column

Sept 2nd   Lieut R.W. Dipey rejoined from 1st Rbn R.F.A

Sept 3rd   Column moved from area K.1 & took over billets of
            3rd D.A.C. in L.25 map Not 57.W
            2/Lt Woodhouse returned from 7 days leave & joined
            D.A.C. on promotion

Sept 8th   Lt Col Leach to England on leave. Command of Colm taken
            over by Capt H.J. Bamford

Sept 10th   104 H.D & 28 S.S wagons sent to adv Horse Transport depot
            this reduces 15pr wagon by half & Howr section by half

Sept 16th   Lieut K.S. Haslam & Lieut R.W. Dipey posted to 3rd Rde from
            E.1. Reinforcement (O.R) posted to exp i from Base

Sept 17th   6 O.R transferred to Bdes

Sept 19th   1,5 O.R transferred to Bdes

Sept 23rd   Lt Col Leach returned from leave & resumed command of Colm

                                                                    HMc

46th Division

121/7/14

46th Div: Ammn Cola

Votnee

Sep 1 15.

Statement

There is nothing special to report. As seen from the Diary many changes in Officers & men have taken place. Discipline has been maintained although constantly changing Section Officers is against it.
All administrative services have been well carried out & supplies ample

1.9.15

R W Leach Lt Col
OC 46th DAC

1/6th B irr Amtn Column — 97
Summary of Events Information

24th Aug   36 OR Transferred to Bdes

21st Aug   Orders received to reduce Establishment
           by 52 OR 104 Hd horses 26 wagons
           5" How 366 Rds 10 p 2,592 Rds

46th Div Amm Column   96
        Summary of Events & Information

4" Aug   Lieuts Vale & Livsey reported & sent on
         to 20th & 1st Trench How Batteries

"6th
Aug   Lieuts Haslam & Pearman Smith joined
         from Base

"8th
Aug   Lieut Train returned to Clm from 2nd Bde

"9th
Aug   Lieut Train to Hospital. Lieut Bellamy
         to 2nd Bde. 2/Lt Whittles to 1st Bde. Lieut P B
         Smith to 3rd Bde
         Lieut Lipey joined from Base

12th
" Aug   Wheeler James R.S.C.M.

"13th
Aug   Capt Lewis to England

"14th
" Aug   Lieut Lowndes returned from 2nd Bde

"15th
Aug   Lieut Train discharged from Hospital

"16th
Aug   Lieut Lipey to 2nd Bde for instruction

"19th
Aug   Lieut Vosses to Clm from on Sick Rest

23rd
" Aug 24 OR joined to Clm from Park

121/6695

46th Division

46th Divl: Ammn Col n
Vol VIII
1 - 31 - 5 - 15

Statement

There is nothing special to report this month. The men have gained in experience, & are now more capable of coping with difficulties which may arise, & are quicker in settling into billets or bivouacs. They have also improved in care of harness & horses.

NCO's have now a better sense of the responsibilities of their position.

The health of men & horses has been good.

Supplies have been ample of all kinds except hay. A certain amount of green fodder has been obtained in lieu of hay shortage, with great benefit to the horses.

There is still an undue prevalence of mud ulcers among the H.D. horses.

E W Leach, Lt Col
OC 46th DAC

46th Div Amm Column
Summary of Events & Information

July 27th Sections II & III new area at L 96 4.3

July 28th Remainder of Column moved into new area

July 29th 2/Lt Whittles rejoined Column from 2nd Bde RFA
    x.   2/Lt Bellamy promoted Lieut w.e.f. 25th Feb 1915

July 31st Lieut Train attached 3rd Bde RFA & 2/Lt Lownds
           attached 2nd Bde RFA for instructions

July 30th F.S.C.M on Dr Goodwin to see IV
   x.

46th Div Amm Column AHC
Summary of Events & Information

July 1st — Lt Col Heath to England on leave. Capt A P Nicol took over command of Amn Tenn

July 6th — Gunners to Bdes for instruction in Gunnery

July 8th — Lt Col Heath returned from leave took over comd of Amn from Capt A P Nicol

July 9th — 7 S C m on W Woods

July 10th — Gun Wordle finished Bdes gone into action. Capt A P Nicol transferred to 4th How Bde AC. Lt R C Frain rejoined column from 20th Trench How Bty

July 12th — Establishment of Amn reduced by 3 GS wagons, 12 Horses 6 to sivers, The whole transferred to 3rd DAC

July 14th — 2/Lt Whittles attached 2nd Bde R F A for instructions

July 16th — Amn visited by Inspector Horse Transport 1st Army

July 21st — Reinforcements joined 12 other Ranks

July 23rd — 2/Lt P B Lambell transferred to 4/1st Trend Mty

July 26th — Capt Lewis transferred to DAC from 4th Rifle Bde

131/6343

46th Division

46th Div: June & July
Vol VI
1-30-7-15

Statement

Except for the move into a new area, the work of the Column has been normal + I have nothing special to report.

The night march to the new billet was satisfactorily carried out.

The condition of the horses has been satisfactory, with only a normal number in the sick lines. If it were not for cases of breaking out on the fetlocks + coronets (mud ulcers) the number of sick would not be more than 2%.

The health of the men has been good
Supplies have been satisfactory
Discipline has been good

R W Leach Lt Col
OC 46th D A C

30. 6. 15

46th Div Ammn Clm
Summary of Events & Information

June 1st Reparation issued to all ranks of D.A.C

June 3rd How portion 46th D.A.C joined temp'y

June 6th F.G.C.M held on D/Shoone & D Shepherd

June 12th Sentence on A/C Shoone & D Shepherd suspended

June 14th BSM Woodward reduced to the ranks
Authority G.O.C H.Q. Corps letter D/2695

June 16th Night route march under Officers Cmdg

June 17th How portion 46th D.A.C rejoined unit

June 23rd Clm left CROIX DE POPERINGHE to take over Billets of 50th DAC at ABEELE

June 30th Lt Col R ? lurch to England on being command of Clm taken over by Capt A.P. Price.

121/5971

46th Division

46th Div: Ammn "Col"

Vol I June 1915.

a/2
a/6

Statement

During the past month the Column has been occupied almost entirely with routine work - issue of Ammunition to Brigade Columns + training - The men have shewn improve- ment both in drill + care of horses -
It has been possible to carry out rifle shooting on a miniature range on most days with satisfactory results
Advantage has been taken of the fine weather to improve the horse lines, + get rid of the accumulation of manure, + also to get a large number of men into bivouacs instead of barns. The latter have in nearly all cases been found to be very verminous -
The horses have been kept in good condition + the proportion of sick has been normal
The discipline has been good
Supplies of all kinds have been quite satisfactory

1. 6. 15

R W Leach Lt Col
OC 46th (4th) DAC

46th Div Amn Column   87
        Summary of Events & Information

26 May   7Lt Ballamy rejoined Clm from 1st Bde R.F.A
         7Lt Lowndes   —   ,   —   2nd Bde R.F.A

27 May   Lt Martin joined 2nd Bde R.F.A for Instructions
         Lt Train   —   —   3rd Bde R.F.A for Instructions

30 May   Rockets received & issued to 137th 138th & 139th Inf Bdes

                                                            HMC

86

May 7th Amtn issued to 2nd 3rd Bde AC & 4th How Bde AC

May 8th Amtn issued to 1st & 2nd Bde & Very lights to 4th [?]
         Lt Middleton A accidently shot himself through leg

May 9th Amtn issued to 1st 2nd & 3rd Bde AC 3 Sections
         turned out to give Assistance at fire on
         DRANOURRE BAILLEUL Road, not required

May 10th Amtn issued to 1st 2nd & 3rd Bde AC

May 11th Amtn issued to 2nd & 3rd Bde AC

May 12th Amtn issued to 1st 2nd Bde AC & 4th How Bde AC
         2/Lt Bellamy attached 1st Bde RFA
         2/Lt Lownds attached 1st Bde RFA for instructions
         Designation of Coln changed to 46th Div Amtn Coln

May 13th Amtn & Grenades to 1st Bde AC

May 14th Amtn issued to 1st 2nd & 3rd Bdes & How Bde AC

May 15th Amtn issued to 2nd Bde Grenades to 2nd & 3rd Bde AC
         Cpl SB & OR joined from Base

May 16th Amtn issued to 1st 2nd & 3rd Bde AC

North Midland Div Amm Clm   85
Summary of Events & Information

May 1 Exercise, Driving Drill 4 teams per section
2 from R C O's & men washing underclothing
under section arrangements. Sentence awarded
by F G C M on G? Lawton & D? Welles promulgated
in accordance with Manual Mil Law
D? Rowley rejoined Clm from 46th Bde F A

May 2 Exercise, Church Parade 11 am amm issued to
2nd & 1st Bde A C and 4th How Bde A C Grenades to 2nd &c

May 3 Exercise, 5 teams from each section to Driving Drill
Amm issued to 1st & 3rd Bde grenades to 1st & 4th How Bde
96 men to Baths at ST. JANS. CAPPEL. Bomb & chg
rejoined from H Q finished 10 day course Telephony

May 4 Exercise with wagons, R/L & punching Drill. Kit
Inspection all NCO's & men amm issued to 3rd & 4th Bdes

May 5 Amm issued to 2nd & 3rd Bde amm clms
Lieutenant J F auer AVC transferred to ADVS
North Mid Div.
Lieut Huston AVC joined and took over duties from
Lt J auer

May 6 Amm & Grenades issued to 3rd & 2nd Bde A C

121/5553/3

46th Division

46th Div: Ammu'n Col'n
Vol III 1 — 30.5.15

but as pointed out in last months statement
careful thought has to be given to the routes
between the DAC & the Bde Columns, on account
of the difficulty of turning the quarter lock
wagons.

Discipline has on the whole been up to standard.
There have been several cases of serious crime, but
the sentences awarded will it is hoped prevent
a recurrence.

Supplies & administrative services have been
very satisfactory.

May 1st 1915

TW Leach Lt Col
OC 1/m DAC

Statement

The position of the column at Croix de Poperinghe has been very favourable for additional training, especially during the latter part of the month when the ground got sufficiently hard to enable driving drill to be carried out in the fields. Hitherto this has been impossible both at home & in this country. Even in the short time available a marked improvement is visible, both in the mens riding, & handling their horses in the team. Rides for Officers & NCO's have been carried out with good results. The condition of the horses is satisfactory although the shortness of bulk food is visible. Straw has been tried as an addition to the hay, but has been given up on account of its liability to produce colic. One horse I regret to state died from it. Oat straw would in all probability be free from this defect, but it is unobtainable. If chaff cutters were available wheat straw might be used chopped with the corn. —

Having a Regular officer as Adjutant has been a great help to me. I am strongly of opinion that every Territorial R.A.C. should have a Regular Officer as its Adjutant.

No difficulty has been experienced, or is anticipated, in the supply of ammunition

North Midland F.A. Amn Column
Summary of Events - Information

April 27, Exercise, Marching Order Section II for Inspection by
O.C., No I Lecture by Adj't, 4 Teams from No 1
Driving Drill, 2pm 6 Teams from No II Driving
Drill, Very Lights issued to 1st & 2nd Bdes [illegible]
No 15 S.S. Bailey H.S. Joined from [illegible]

April 28th Exercise Driving Drill 8 teams from I & II Sections
7 S.C.M. S.M. Lawton & Dr Willis Afternoon Driving
Drill 8 teams each from III & IV

April 29 Exercise, Driving Drill 8 teams from III & IV
Afternoon Driving Drill 8 teams each from
I & II Amtn issued to 1st Bde [illegible]
[illegible] to 2nd & 3rd Bdes [illegible]
Dr Manning Sec II 15[?] [illegible] Sec I [illegible]
to form [illegible]
Amtn issued to 2nd Bde Grenades to 2nd & 3rd Bdes

April 30 Exercise, Driving Drill 8 teams each from
I & II 6.30 A.M. N.C.O. ride S. Lawton &
Dr Willis retired by 7 S.C.M. first trial
illegal Afternoon Driving Drill III & IV
Very lights issued to 2nd Bde Detonators
issued to Notts & Derby H[illegible]

North Midland Div'n Am'tn Column
Summary of Events & Information

April 12 — Exercise No I with wagons remainder without Section parades 9am N C O's ride 10.35 am N° III Sec inspection of boots & clothing by O C 2pm Classifying of Horses for scale of feeds by A.D.V.S

April 13 — Exercise, marching orders with wagons Section III Inspection by O C N C O's ride Am'tn & Grenades issued to 1st 2nd & 3rd Bde NCO Afternoon inspection by O C I IV + H Q Sections Boots & Clothing Instructions in Harness Fitting N.C.O's. 40 men Baths at BAILLEUL

April 14 — Exercise II Section N C O's ride marching order with wagons Inspection by O C Grenades & Am'tn issued to 2nd & 3rd Bde N C B NCO's & gun carriers [illegible]

April 15 — Exercise Church Parade B C parties [illegible] Afternoon Baths for 40 men remainder section arrangements 16 men formed party Baths

April 16 — Exercise II III & IV NC's marching order for NCO's driving drill Section by Adjt N° I Section [illegible] under Section Off 2pm N.C.O's redrilling 1st 2nd 3rd [illegible] issued

North Midland Div April Column
Summary of Events & Information

April 18 Exercise R.C. church Parade [illegible] men washing and clothing 3 open air & church parade

April 19 Exercise N⁰ II with wagons remainder without R C O' side [illegible] ... 2/pm instruction in gun fitting Officer [illegible] ...

April 20 Exercise N⁰ II with wagons remainder without R C O' side [illegible] ...

April 21 Exercise No II with wagons remainder [illegible] ...
About 6 pm natives reported Soldier in farm about 400 yds from Column Arrested & handed over to A.P.M

79

North Midland Divisional Ammn Column
Summary of Events and Information

April 15 Exercise No I Section with wagons remained
without Grenades and Ammn issued to 1st & 3rd
Bde Ammn Cols, Afternoon All N.C.O. + men
Semaphore Signalling Offrs Coy visited
4th DAC to enquire Whts working under
the amalgamation of lorries + wagons
R P arranged with Road to be at junction
of roads on S.L. Map 7 + 8 B also Sheet 26 SW

April 16 Exercise No I with wagons remained without
Grenades Ammn issued to 1st Bde DAC Ammn
issued to Howitzer Bde A.C. 2pm N.C.O.s H.Q. NCOs
and men lecture under Bombr remainder rifle drill
Officer On dy examined all units supply and
report to Col H. NCOs of III. Riding drill
6 pm Officer doing matters together under O.C.
100 men to leave on 2 days lve

April 17 Exercise No III with wagons remained without
10.30 am NCOs ride Exercise issued to 1st & 2nd
3rd Bde Amm Coln to 3rd Bde AC Afternoon
All N.C.O. + men Semaphore
B.S.M Nicholson posted from II to I Rdg Sch
Sgt Wilkinson from II to I

North Mid Divisional Amn Column
Summary of Events and Information

April 12 Section [?] to stand by ready to move
          from ...

April 13 At 11:10pm 12/4/15 instructions received for
          Heavy portion of No IV Section to proceed at 5:30AM
          13th inst & join 28th Div Amn Clm 1 mile
          EAST of POPERINGHE they marched out under
          2/Lt C A Duke Walker Strength 1 Offr 16 men
          H D [?] and 4 wagons. About 11:35pm 12th
          sentry reported Zeppelin over column it was
          flying S towards BAILLEUL on which it dropped
          Bombs afterwards returning NE towards ... ...
          Officer Cmdg estimated height to be from 15,000
          to 2,000 feet. Exercise before breakfast under
          Section Cmdrs. Afternoon marching & rifle
          drill, usual issue of SAA & Grenades and
          ... ... How Bde Clm

April 14 Exercise ... ... side arms Route to be taken
          when delivering Amn to Brigade Columns
          Section on Harness fitting & all N C Os
          men not on duty 2/Lt ... R.P. ... to
          ST JANS C APPEL

77

North Midland Divisional Ammn Column

April 10 — At 12.30 am message received from 1st Bde Ammn Colm asking for the RA3 [?] wagons to be sent urgent. This was dispatched at once. 1st Sect were attached [?] armed of [?] took over Billets of 5th NAC at LA POTARIERE arriving about 1.30 pm. No III Section from ST JANS CAPPEL moved into Section Houses from 4th D.A.C. had arrived earlier. S.A.A. was issued to 3rd Bde A.C. Lamps, Sights & Reminders were issued to 1st, 2nd and 3rd Bde C.M.C. [?]

April 11 — Church Parade at 9.0 am taken by [?] Ammn issued to 1st and 3rd Bde Ammn Colm. Some time was been spent in topping [?] up water troughs from old casings. No water supply here is not good. 9.15 pm 6 H.D. & 1 B. arrived from N.M.Cav Squadron. Here Secret orders [?] showing line to be taken up in case of [?]

April 12 — [?] orders [?] General Policy [?] 100 men went to [?] at [?] Inspection of horses by A.D.V.S. [?] Reminders issued to 1st, 2nd & 3rd Bde A.C. orders received No. IV

North Midland Divisional Am'n Col'n
Summary of events & information

1915	
April 6	under Section arrangements. A.C. ovn. 17 men under S/Lt E. the Baker musketry at reindeer range. Rifle Rally for Rum
April 7	Exercise in morning, 1st Bde sent in Ordy to report they had moved. musketry under S/Lt Bellamy (7 men) Ofr Commdg checked all 15 pr Amtn
April 8	18 wagon proceeded to refilling point and exchanged with Am'n Park 2546 Fuzes & 1847 Shell, remainder Exercise, Afternoon No III Section shifted their lines to Field left by No II Section 17 men musketry under R.S.M Hornby Officer Commdg visited with O.C Sections the Billets to be taken over from 5th L.A.C 5.20pm Despatch received from C R.A to say 5th L.A.C move on the 10th & we take over
April 9	Marching Order under Section Cmdrs, Amtn issued to 1st Bde A.C & to R.F.A 17 men musketry under Capt Nicol Amtn issued to 2nd Bde A.C both Mid R.F.A

	North Midland Divisional Ammuⁿ Clm	
Date	Summary of Events & Information	Remarks
April 4	on miniature Range 2 pm 2/Lt R Whittle proceeded with SAA portion of II Section to join Lt R.C Fram. 1 O/r 25 OR 4 R 30 HD wagons the whole of N° II Section now away. 2.30 pm Church Parade. Received a new Censor Stamp N° 325 old one destroyed.	
April 5	Marching Order with wagons under Section Commd^{rs} Afternoon 17 men under 2/Lt G.G Lourades musketry on miniature range. Lt Col R.P Leach visited advance section, roads thereabouts not good At 11/15 pm orders received to move to C^p DE POPERINGE on 10th April	at ST JANSCAPPEL
April 6	18 wagons sent to 1st Bde N.M.R.F.A ammun Clm to exchange Fuzes left at 12 am returned 5.45 pm Captⁿ H.J Banford reported he had to go to Batteries direct and Ammuⁿ Colmⁿ after, loss of time officer of Batteries could not state definitely ... ... authority received from C.R.A to change all doubtful Fuzes in 1st 2nd & 3rd Bde A.C N.M.R.F.A Officer Commdg proceeded to C^p DE POPERINGE to inspect billets &c OC 5th D.A.C reported he would not be starting until 11th Marching Orders with wagons not	

75

North Midland Divisional Ammunition Column.

Date	Summary of Events & Information.	Remarks
1915. April 1	Sections parades in morning. 2nd Lieut. Savory arrived in the afternoon, and took up the duties of adjutant, in place of 2nd Lieut. Ballamy.	
April 2nd	Marching Order in morning under Section Officers. Parade for all N.C.O's in afternoon lecture by Adjutant. The S.A.A section under 2/Lt G.G Lowndes returned to column from 2nd Cav Division, reported two H D horses short one Shot, one taken over by Mobile Veterinary Section	
April 3	Exercise in morning Orders received to send 15pr portion of II Section to Farm on ST JANS CAPPEL – BERTHEN road 200 yards W of Church S side of road. 15 men had shooting practice on miniature range. At 2pm Lt R.C Frain proceeded with 15pr portion of II Section to ST JANS CAPPEL – BERTHEN road, consisting of 51 men 5 R & 5 8 H D wagons. men inoculated the second time	
April 4	Exercise in morning Baths arranged for men 12 men under 2/Lt P B Dumbell Shooting Practice	

121/5254

4b. btn Div l'Armata Col.
Vol III 1— 30.4.15

their condition well although they were five days on board ship without any chance of getting rid of the droppings. —

Nearly all the wagons of this Column are of the Mk X type, as far as my limited experience allows I very much question its suitability for service in this country on account of its only leaving a quarter lock. The full lock type of a lighter pattern would appear to me more suitable. I can imagine many cases in which delay in ammunition supply might occur owing to wagons being unable to reverse in a moderately wide road.

March 31st 1915

R W Leach Lt Col
OC 2/m D.A.C.

71

The Discipline has been good — a small amount of insubordination to NCO's, but no drunkenness or absence.

All the Administrative Services have been quite satisfactory — The food supply has been regular & ample, & no difficulty has been experienced in obtaining supplies of fresh vegetables — The men have had quite as good billets as could possibly be expected on Active Service

The Column is now complete in its establishment of horses; the last batch of Remounts received on 28th inst being of very good quality & up to the standard of the other horses of the Column.

I would suggest — as a result of my experience of our embarkation that the order for horses to carry nosebags with feeds on their necks be cancelled. In many cases it started abcesses under the strap of the nose bag, rendering the draught horses useless for some time as the harness neck bands could not be put on. In all the cases where an abcess did form, it was of a deep seated nature taking a long time to heal. The horses kept

Statement.

The Training of the Column has been continued during the month as far as possible, & the results have been satisfactory. The NCO's & men have all benefitted by having to work under conditions altogether different from service at home. Although there is much still to be learnt I hope that all ranks are now sufficiently trained to enable the work required of them to be carried out with credit. Independence has been learnt & the men have accustomed themselves readily to the altered conditions.

During the last few days I have had the assistance of the Adjutant of the VI.th Div.l Ammn. Column. He has been of the greatest service to me, & I shall be able to work on lines which have been found in the VI.th Div.l to stand the test of war. I would suggest similar help being given to any other Column coming out from England. The Field Service Regulations do not and cannot give sufficient information, & much that is laid down in the official books is inapplicable. More can be learnt in a few days from an officer who has had experience than from any amount of study of books.

Mar. 28	Church parade at 9 a.m. A mounted party under Capt. Nicol proceeded to Caestre to fetch 3 riding and 42 H.D. horses. 14 H.D. were handed over to the 4th (How.) Section at Meteren, and 5 to the Lincoln & Leicester Inf. Brigade.
Mar. 29.	Brigade route march at 9 a.m. Lecture to Section Commanders & senior Sergeants at 12 noon by Capt. Dundas. Sentence of 2 months F.P. No 2, passed by F.G.C.M. on Dr. Corbishley, H, was promulgated at 2 p.m. Special order issued as to branding of horses.
Mar. 30.	Exercise of horses in morning. Harness cleaning and stables in afternoon. The Section Commdrs, Adjt, and senior Sergeants proceeded with Capt. Dundas to the 6th D.A.C. to observe their method of working. Special orders issued about Roll Calls, and the checking of stores on wagons.
Mar. 31.	Route march under Section Officers. Ammunition issued in afternoon to 1st, 2nd, & 3rd Bde Amm. Cols. Special orders issued about Sick, Rifles, & Branding of Horses. H.W. Bellamy, 2 Lieut & Acting Adjt N.M.D.A.C.

Near Le Veronier,
31-3-15.

Mar.24 (cont'd)	Special orders issued about Drinking Water, Sick Parade, and Pay. At 9 p.m. a man in R.F.A. uniform was arrested talking to a sentry; he was unable to give any account of himself.
Mar.25	Column route march at 9 a.m. Ammunition again taken by Sect. II to the Batteries in action. More men were inoculated. The man arrested the previous evening was sent to MERRIS with an escort, and handed over to the A.P.M.
Mar.26	The D.D.R. came at 8.30 a.m., and asked if 58 light draught horses could be taken in place of the 29 H.D. asked for. It was explained that this could not be done owing to lack of personnel. The D.D.R. therefore wired for 29 H.D. horses to be sent. Exercise of horses in morning. Stables and harness cleaning in afternoon. Special orders issued about Sick Horses, Sentries, Fuzes, and Firewood.
Mar.27	Capt. Dundas, 6th D.A.C., attached to the Column, arrived at 9.0 a.m. A court martial was held at 10 a.m. on Dr. Corbishley (Hdqrs. Staff) for theft.

Mar. 21 (contd)	In the afternoon arrangements were made for all the men to have a bath. A special return of all S.A.A. in possession of unit was rendered. Special orders issued as to Bounds.
Mar. 22	Column route march at 9 a.m. In the afternoon the D.D.R. inspected the horses of the Column, & expressed his satisfaction with their condition. Arrangements were made for deficiencies (1 R I and 29 H.D.) to be made up, and for mares in foal to be replaced. Special orders issued as to Cameras, Newly-Sown Fields, and Rifles (not to be carried on wagons).
Mar. 23	Column route march at 9 a.m. The A.D.V.S. visited the lines in the afternoon, and gave instructions with regard to the laying of brick standings for the horses. Special order issued about Inoculation.
Mar. 24	Exercise of horses in morning. Ammunition was taken up by Sections I & IV to the Batteries (one per Brigade R.F.A. and Heavy Battery) attached to 6ª Division. Men of the Column were inoculated.

Mar.17 (cont'd)	the main road was cleared, and the wagons could be got out quickly in either direction.
Mar.18	The C.O. attended a conference at Div. Artilly Headquarters at 9.0 a.m. A route march took place in the afternoon, a short route of about 3 miles being taken. The following routine orders were issued – Reveille 5.45: Stables – 6.0: breakfast 7.0: morning parade – 8.45, by which time all men to be washed and shaved.
Mar.19	Route marches under Section Officers in morning. Stables and harness cleaning in afternoon. Snow had fallen during the night, making the side of the roads extremely soft for the wagons.
Mar.20	Exercise of horses in morning. Stables & harness cleaning in afternoon. Special order issued with regard to Drinking Water, and Deficiencies in Equipment.
Mar. 21	Inspection by O.C. at 9 a.m. Immediately after, by order received from Div! Headquarters, the wagons of Sections 2 & 3 were brought out from the side road when they had been placed, and were parked again on the STEENWERCK – LEVERRIER road.

March 13 (cont'd)	2nd Cavalry Div. Amm. Col. They left at 3 p.m. No orders received about moving.
March 14	Parade for inspection by C.O. at 10 a.m., followed by exercise of horses. Section IV (Heavies), & remainder of Section I, ordered to be ready to join 6th Div. Amm. Col.
March 15	Exercise of horses in morning. Musketry instruction in afternoon.
March 16	The following details left at 6 a.m. to join 6th Div. Amm. Col :— the 15-pr portion of Sect. I, 1 officer, 54 men, 56 horses, 13 wagons: Sect. IV (Heavies) 1 officer, 20 men, 21 horses, 5 wagons. Exercise of horses in morning. The remaining part of Sect. IV (Howitzers), 21 men, 17 horses, 5 wagons was sent to METEREN to 4th Div. Amm. Col. in the afternoon.
March 17	The details attached to 6th Division returned in the morning. Exercise of horses in morning; musketry & signalling in afternoon. The wagons were parked on the side-roads leading into the STEENWERCK — LEVERRIER road. In this way

March 10 (cont'd)	for the Column to be ready to move: horses to be exercised near lines. At 3 p.m. a "practice turn-out" in marching order took place.
Special orders issued as to Alarm Posts, and challenging of motor-cars.
March 11	The G.O.C. Division paid a visit at 9.30 a.m. and addressed the officers and men of the Column. Orders were received to move off at 1 p.m. The Column marched by Flêtre & Bailleul to the Steenwerck - Le Verrier road, W. of 5-road junction, arriving 6.45 p.m. A billeting party had been sent on, and the Column was billeted along the above road.
March 12	Orders received for the Column to be ready to move at an hour's notice. The side roads around were reconnoitred to ascertain by what routes the column could move. Lt. Martin, 11 men, 14 horses, and 3 wagons proceeded with the remaining 5" Howitzer ammunition to 4th Div. Amm. Col. at METEREN.
March 13	2 Lt. Lowndes, 29 men, 32 horses and 7 S.A.A. wagons from Sect. I were detailed to join

March 7	Reveille 7.0. During the morning the wagons were parked on the main road Cassel — St. Omer. A billeting party of 2 officers & 7 N.C.O,s was sent to Caestre to find billets for the Column. Lieut. Martin returned and reported that 22 men, 33 horses, and 8 wagons of Sec. IV (Howitzers) had been taken over by the 4th Division Ammunt. Column.
March 8	The horses were exercised and harness inspected in the morning. A man was arrested as a spy, but the interpreter found on examination that he was a French official forester. Orders received for Column to proceed next day to Caestre.
March 9.	Reveille 5.0. The Column marched by Staple and Le Boreande to Caestre, arriving 12.0 noon. The wagons were parked on the CAESTRE - STRAZEELE road. The water supply was poor, and search was made for a better supply, without much result.
March 10	During the morning, horse-rugs, great-coats, and surplus kits were handed in. Orders were received

March 4 (contd)	equipment were made up, & rations drawn for 2 days. Le Comte de Rousseau joined the Column as interpreter. The Column entrained by sections, Headquarters & Section I leaving at 11.20 p.m.
March 5	The remaining sections left Harn as follows:— Sect. II at 1.20 a.m.; Sect. III at 3.0 a.m.; Sect. IV at 7.30 a.m. Two stops were made on the way for watering horses, &c. The stops were in most cases too short for watering to be properly carried out. Sect. I reached CASSEL station at 9.0 p.m., detrained, & proceeded to billets already found for them at Crève Coeur Farm.
March 6	Sect. III & IV arrived at CASSEL stn. at 4.0 a.m. & 8.0 a.m. respectively; Sect. II at 4.0 a.m. at HAZEBROUCK. All proceeded to CRÈVE COEUR. Lieut. Martin was at once sent with 8 wagons of Howitzer Ammunition to 4th Division Ammunt Col. at Meteren. Ammunition to complete to War Establishment was sent up from Ammunt Park.

North Midland Divisional Ammunition Column.

Date	Summary of Events & Information.	Remarks
1915.		
March 1st	Column, less Headquarters & Sect. IV (Heavies), on board S.S. Archimedes: Headqrs & Sect IV (Heavies) on S.S. Caledonia; both at Southampton. Routine on board ship — Reveille 6.0; Stables 6.30; Clean decks, stables, & men's quarters, 9.0 a.m. & 5.30 p.m.; morning & afternoon stables; ½ hr. foot-drill on quay in afternoon. No officer or man allowed off ship after 4.30 p.m. Lights out 9.15 p.m. Special orders issued as to sanitation & roll-calls.	
March 2	Routine as above. The ships did not leave the quay. Rations drawn for two more days.	
March 3.	Routine as above. Collision stations practised. S.S. Caledonia sailed at 6 p.m., the Archimedes at 7.30 p.m.	
March 4	The ships reached Havre at 10.30 a.m. The Column at once disembarked, and concentrated in Halls 3. 13 Horses were cast & replaced. Deficiencies in clothing, &	

N. M. Division

1st N.M. Div: Ammun Coln
Vol II 1 – 31.3.15
Nil

www.ingramcontent.com/pod-product-compliance
Lightning Source LLC
Chambersburg PA
CBHW082011220426
43670CB00014B/2601